BERLITZ®

INDIA

How to use our guide

These 256 pages cover the **highlights** of India, grouped into five regions. Although not exhaustive, our selection of sights will enable you to make the best of your trip.

The **sights** to see are described on pages 59 to 191. Those most highly recommended are pinpointed by the Berlitz traveller symbol.

For **general background** see the sections India and the Indians (p. 8), Facts and Figures (p. 19), History (p. 20), and the section Religions of India (p. 50).

Entertainment and **activities** (including eating out) are described on pages 192 to 217.

The **practical information,** hints and tips you will need for your trip begin on page 218. This section is arranged alphabetically with a list for easy reference.

The **map section** at the back of the book (pp. 244-252) will help you find your way around and locate the principal sights.

Finally, if there is anything you cannot find, look in the complete **index** (pp. 253-256).

Text: Jack Altman
Staff Editor: Christina Jackson
Photography: Walter Imber
Layout: Doris Haldemann
Cartography: Falk-Verlag, Hamburg

Printed in Switzerland by Weber SA, Bienne.

7th edition (1995/1996)

CONTENTS

CONTENTS

CONTENTS

Although we make every effort to ensure the accuracy of the information in this guide, changes do occur. If you have any new information, suggestions or corrections to contribute, we would like to hear from you. Please write to Berlitz Publishing at one of the addresses on p. 2.

Acknowledgements
We wish to express our warmest thanks to the Government of India Tourist Office, in particular KB Singh, Asha Malhotra and Kamla Bhatnagar, as well as to Air India and Indian Airlines, for their help in the preparing this guide. We are also grateful to Valerie Dixon, S. Makhija, Kim Gordon-Bates, Adrienne Jackson, Afzal Friese, Vinita Schürch and Arun Pabari for their invaluable assistance.

Cover photo: Taj Mahal

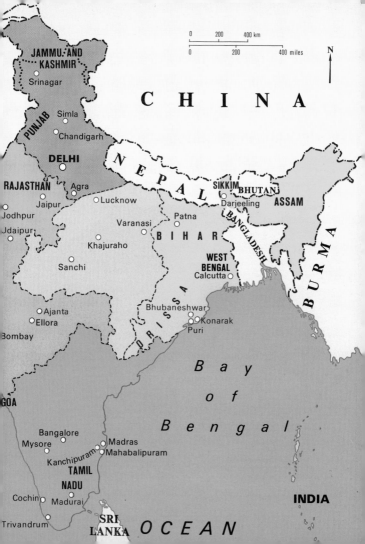

INDIA AND THE INDIANS

This land is a constant challenge to mind and body, a glorious shock to the system. It is no place for the faint-hearted. India is exhilarating, exhausting and infuriating – a land where you'll find the harsh, but equally often cheerful practicalities of daily life overlay the mysteries that popular myth attaches to India. In place of the much publicised, and much misunderstood mysticism of its ancient religions, the reality of India has quite another magic to offer: in the sheer profusion of its peoples and landscapes.

There *is* one India. It derives its strength from the diamond-shaped

subcontinent which stretches over 3,000 km (1,800 miles) from the Kashmir mountains in the north right down to Cape Comorin on the Indian Ocean.

From east to west India covers 3,000 km from Arunachal Pradesh and Assam on the border with its neighbours China and Burma to the Gujarat coast on the Arabian Sea.

Only in more recent post-colonial times did its natural geography exclude the countries of Pakistan and Bangladesh. Even there, for all

A whole world separates Bihari rice-workers from this Rajasthani camel-boy, but India unites them.

the perennial hostilities, there's an undeniable cultural affinity with India – feuding brothers rather than unrelated strangers.

In fact, when you look at its 4,000 years of history – or any of today's newspapers, for that matter – its countless feuds seem to be a perpetual but necessary dynamic of Indian civilization.

It's a massive family, with a lot of different and inevitably conflicting regional and sectarian interests. Pick up a rupee banknote and you have the money printed in India's 15 official languages: Hindi, Urdu, Sanskrit, Sindhi, Bengali, Marathi, Gujurati, Oriya, Punjabi, Asamese, Kashmiri, Malayalam, as well as Kannada, Tamil, and Telugi. A total count of the many languages spoken all over India, leaving out the dialects, came to 1,652, written in 13 different alphabets.

The national language of Hindi, is spoken by less than the majority, and English, for which the government has a permanent programme of modernization, is spoken by just 3 percent of the people, most in the leading cities. Everybody 'speaks' cricket, though, with its jargon of *innings, wickets* and *boundaries* in every dialect.

One of the first impressions you'll get at the airport in Delhi or Bombay is the diversity of ethnic types. From blue-eyed and sometimes red-haired Kashmiris and the Chinese-Tibetans from Sikkim or Darjeeling, through all the shades of coffee of the heartland, right down to dark-skinned, often curly-haired, Dravidians from southern India, you soon realize there's no such thing as a 'typical' Indian.

India's prehistoric settlers were probably what anthropologists call Proto-Australoids. They've since been joined by Mongols, Aryans, Greeks, Arabs, Turks, Persians and Afghans, while Dutch and British, Portuguese and French have also left their traces.

The landscape is alternately rich and arid, lush and grim. In the north the snow-bound Himalayas make an appropriate home for the Hindu gods. Kashmir is a serenely beautiful and coveted land of green forest, alpine meadows and lakes, while the Punjab in the north-west is the fertile centre of the country's

The Jain faith is as intricate as the maze of pillars in this temple on Mount Abu.

Green Revolution, helping to make the nation self-sufficient in wheat, barley and millet. On the doorstep of this wealth, the Thar Desert of noble Rajasthan heralds the vast Deccan plateau of parched ruddy granite that dominates the peninsula of southern India.

Delhi stands at the western end of the Ganga (Ganges) river basin in which India grows much of its rice. This new name was created under the 'Re-indianization' which followed Independence, and others have also been affected: Kanpur is now Cawnpore, Pune is Poona, and Varanasi is Benares, for example.

Flanked with occasional forest leading up into the foothills of the Himalayas, the flat plain stretches right across to the Bay of Bengal 1,600 km (1,000 miles) away, but some are kept as nature reserves for the country's wildlife, notably its tigers, leopards and elephants. Bengal's greenery is the threshold to the tea-plantations of Darjeeling and Assam.

The rugged southern peninsula is hemmed in by low-lying mountains – the Vindhya and Satpura to the north and the Western and Eastern Ghats running parallel to the coasts. The Malabar coast in the west is forested, and sown with crops of coconut, betelnut, pepper, rubber and cashewnut which today still tempt ships across the Arabian Sea. Some of the palm trees here serve to provide shade for beach-resorts in Goa and Kerala.

India's landscape also features man-made architectural treasures, bearing witness to the many great religions and secular civilizations which have enriched the country – monuments now preserved by the restoration programme started by the Archaeological Survey of India after centuries of neglect.

The variety of sights is endless: the Hindu *gopuram* tower-gates of the south, the temples of Varanasi (Benares) the cave-monasteries of Ajanta and Ellora, the beautiful and erotic sculptures of Khajuraho, the splendid marble palaces, fortresses and mausoleums of the emperors and maharajas in Delhi, Agra and Rajasthan, the colonial government buildings in New Delhi or the bizarre style of the Gothic-Oriental railway station in Bombay.

The cities' shanty-town districts are often to be found squatting in the shadow of the shining sky-scrapers, which their residents have been hired to build and where the women carry bricks on their heads as gracefully as a pitcher of water. The women are also responsible for one other characteristic of Indian 'architecture' – cow-dung patties preserved and kept for fuel and artfully shaped into mounds with shapes that differ from region to region, some of them resembling a Buddhist stupa, a Hindu *gopuram* or even a Moslem minaret.

The only constant in this huge landscape is the people themselves. Even in the vast open spaces of the Rajasthan desert or the Deccan plateau of central India, figures pop up from nowhere, a tribesman on camel-back or lone woman holding her headdress in her teeth to keep out the dust as she carries on her head a huge pitcher of water or a stack of firewood. If, as the road stretches before you, empty and clear right up to the horizon, and you can see only the one tree, it's a pretty safe bet you'll find at least one half-naked *sadhu* (holy man) resting in its shade.

The teeming millions living in Calcutta and Bombay have become legendary. They crowd each other into the roadway, bulge out of tiny auto-rickshaws and perch on top of buses and trains; a family of four

or five clings onto a motor-scooter, and a whole schoolclass on one bullock-cart. It's hazardous, buses do topple over, rooftop passengers on trains do occasionally get swept off the top by an overhanging steel rod, but they accept the risk for the free ride – rooftoppers aren't in the habit of buying tickets.

You'll soon become aware of the special genius Indians have acquired in these trying conditions for filling every available space – everyone learns to sit when neccessary on just one buttock. It's a useful knack to acquire if you should venture out on a bus or train, and you will quickly learn to accept, not just the sight of so many people all around you, but also their touch, their smell, and their many and unabashed snorts and belches.

It's important to remember not to apply Western values to everything you see here. The poverty, for instance, does not create the sense of shame as it does for people who live in Western countries. In India poverty is borne with considerable dignity and even with a cheerfulness that some may find difficult to understand. The same form applies to jostling, which is a whole way of life in this country.

INDIA AND THE INDIANS

Everyone makes way for the cow, sacred to the Hindus. The cow has right of way everywhere, either walking nonchalantly through the centre of a city, or reclining across a new expressway. After a while you may begin to detect something other-worldly about the way a cow seems to look around and beyond her immediate surroundings – it's as if she *knows* that she's sacred.

You can't get around it, India is a country where religion is ever present. Anthropologists and historians, theologians, thinkers on all sides, each has a pet explanation for it. The answer is enormously complex, but one factor is almost certainly, quite simply, the weather. India just seems to have *more* of it. The heat rises to its most intense, particularly from April to mid-June, and can try the very limits of human endurance, even among the Indians themselves. The powerful rains of the monsoon (from mid-June to September) are seen as a divine blessing when they come,

How many incarnations have this family known to achieve such wistful melancholy?

14

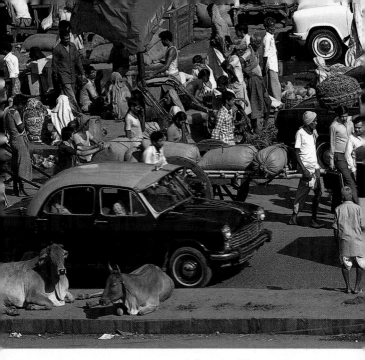

but they don't always come, or they come late, or there is too little or too much. The disaster of flood or drought is perennial, and in the milder times, no doubt the sages ponder these extremes.

Hinduism, embraces more than 83 percent of the population, and is more a way of life than a religion. Its sacred ritual and observances are only a small part of what good

Calcutta's millions are always on the move, but there's not enough room to hurry.

Hindus consider makes them good Hindus for much more than the mystical elements which fascinate and draw so many Westerners to travel here, Hinduism is concerned with the nuts and bolts, that is the

16

Even today the intricate Hindu caste-system, despite the numerous anti-discrimination statutes passed since Independence, still governs for most Indians their choice of job and spouse, friends and, nowadays, political party. Brahmans, that is the priestly caste, fill many of the top posts in the universities and administration; many Indian Army officers can trace their ancestry to the proud *kshatriya* warrior-caste; business is dominated by the merchant or *vaishya* caste; and *shudras* till the land. Untouchables have greater opportunities now to rise on the social scale, a few of them becoming captains of industry or cabinet ministers, but it's still their brethren who sweep the streets.

Most marriages in India are still arranged with carefully negotiated dowries, but if ever more matrimonial advertisements in the weekend editions of *The Times of India* and other equally newspapers mention 'caste no bar', just as many specify the required caste or insist on a 'fair-complexioned' bride, while touting a university diploma and an American work-permit.

Over 80 million Moslems form the second-largest religious group in India – almost as many as the

basics of everyday life: birth, work, health,relationships and death, and all of this being helped along by regular consultations with a local astrologer – a popular practice with industrialists and goat-herds alike – and married with a relaxed attitude to one or more of the millions of gods in the Hindu pantheon, cursing or worshipful according to how well things are going.

17

population of Pakistan – most of the, descendants from Hindu converts of the Mughals' empire, who bore the brunt of Hindu retaliation for long years of subjection and an often unfair, identification with British rule.

Left behind by the exodus to Pakistan at the 1947 partition, they make up the peasantry in the north, and while they mostly take a low profile, you may hear of 'communal incidents' in the cities between the Hindus and Moslems.

Sikhs make up just 2 percent of the population. This comes from their obligation to wear a beard and turban. They drive most of the taxis in Delhi and provide the country's most talented mechanics. With the consistent militant need to defend their faith, they make up a fiercely competent élite in the Indian Army, but they are also skilled farmers at the spearhead of the Green Revolution in the Punjab where most of them live. Their rights have been the source of conflicts in the central government.

Indian Christians, some being descended from Syrians that came to India, or from those converted by British and Portuguese missionaries, number about 19 million.

Buddhism almost disappeared in India after the invasions of the 7th century, but has made a comeback for its appeal to Untouchables as an escape from discrimination. There are now more than 5 million, many of them in Maharashtra.

The Jains' non-violent religion excludes them from agriculture as a profession, but they dominate the electronics industry in Bangalore. The tiny, but powerful community of Parsis brought Zoroastrianism from Iran and its people shine in business today.

The new religion of India is of course Modernization, and Young Upwardly Mobile Professionals are everywhere. Growing involvement in electronics, telecommunications, nuclear power and space satellites is intended to take the country, as one official said, 'directly from the 19th into the 21st century'.

To achieve this, the government is cutting through bureaucracy to break with political corruption and find some kind of peaceful *modus vivendi* for communal and regional interests. Former US ambassador John Kenneth Galbraith called it a 'functioning anarchy'. The miracle of how it functions is well worth watching.

FACTS AND FIGURES

Geography:	India's area of 3,287,593 sq km (1,269,246 sq miles) makes it the 7th largest country in the world. It stretches 3,220 km (2,012 miles) from Kashmir south to Cape Comorin on the Indian Ocean, and 2,980 km (1,848 miles) from the eastern frontier with China and Burma to the Gujarat coast on the Arabian Sea. The Himalayas mark the northern frontier, leading down to the plain of the Ganga river stretching east to the Bay of Bengal. In the north-east, Cherrapunji holds the record for the world's heaviest rainfall in a single year, 22,990 mm (905 inches) in 1861. The triangular Deccan plateau of the southern peninsula is flanked by the Vindhya and Satpura mountains to the north and the Eastern and Western Ghats which run parallel to the Coromandel and Malabar coasts. Highest mountain: Kanchenjunga (Sikkim) 8,586 m (28,168 ft)
Population:	844 million, of whom 72% are Indo-Aryan, mostly in north, 25% Dravidian in south, 3% others. Density is 267 people per square kilometre (670 per square mile).
Capital:	Delhi (pop. 8,370,000).
Major cities:	Bombay (pop. 12,572,000), Calcutta (pop. 10,860,000), Hyderabad (pop. 4,280,000), Bangalore (pop. 4,087,000), Madras (pop. 5,360,000), Ahmedabad (pop. 3,280,000), Pune (pop. 2,440,000), and Kanpur (pop. 2,1101,000).
Government:	India is a republic of 25 states, with seven union territories governed from Delhi. A member of the Commonwealth, it has parliamentary government established by the 1950 constitution. The President has limited responsibility, real power being vested in a Prime Minister and Council of Ministers responsible to the 544 members of the Lok Sabha (House of the People). State government is in the hands of Chief Ministers and State legislatures, which is represented centrally by a 244-member Rajya Sabha (the Council of States).
Religion:	83% Hindu, 11% Moslem, 2.5% Christian, 2% Sikh, 1.5% Buddhist, Jain and others.

HISTORY

India has always been a hodge-podge of peoples.

Apart from some pre-Ice Age hominids, the first settlers to arrive in India were Negritos and Proto-Australoids. Migrants of Mediterranean stock from the Middle East and Asia seem to have made up the Dravidians, now principally in the southern peninsula.

In 4000 BC agriculturalists made their first appearance up in the hills of Baluchistan in the north-west. In the Indus river valley, improved techniques permitted the storage of wheat and barley beyond daily needs, and so the cities of Harappa and Mohenjodaro emerged in the year 2300 BC, creating a civilization even more advanced than that of the Aryans who came later.

The sewage system and houses outside the citadel were better constructed than their modern equivalents, and among their animals was a major Indian contribution to the world's cuisine – the chicken.

Modern archaeology suggests that this Indus Valley civilization was destroyed not by Aryan conquerors, but by Indus river floods when it changed course, perhaps due to earthquake, about 1700 BC.

The Hindus' Ancestors

The Aryans arrived on the scene some 200 years later. Originally from Russia or Asia, they migrated to Mesopotamia first and then on to Iran before entering India. These fair-skinned cattle-breeders, who saw the cow as an especially sacred animal, cultivated agriculture in the Punjab after waging war against the Dasas, who then became their slaves.

Early events surrounding the Indo-Aryans can be deduced from the later writings of the *Rig-Veda* (priestly hymns), *Puranas* (ancient tales of kings and gods) and the epic poems of the *Mahabharata* and *Ramayana*. These provided the basis for Hinduism, and the epics' heroic battles (see p. 171) suggest there was a prolonged struggle for land-rights over the fertile plains north and east of modern Delhi, followed by invasions and wars.

If ancient writings give only a romanticized view, they do offer a more precise picture of Indo-Aryan society. Their long wars against the indigenous people established their leaders as kings with a hereditary divinity, which the *Brahmans* (the priests) exchange for a privileged position of their own.

The caste-system was already taking shape. Before the conquests, the Aryans were organized in three classes: warriors, priests and commoners. Then they established four distinct categories known as *varna*, literally 'colour'.

As possessors of magical power associated with ritual sacrifice and sacred utterance, Brahmans were the sole interpreters of the Vedic scriptures. They laid down a social pecking-order with themselves in first place, followed by *Kshatriyas* (the warriors), *Vaishyas* (cultivators or traders) and *Shudras* (serfs and those of mixed blood).

This organisation became more elaborate as the division of labour became more complicated, so the growing number of occupational groups were subsequently defined as *jati* (subcastes), often living in separate villages. Each caste would preserve its 'purity' by avoiding intermarriage and not sharing food with other castes. Outside these were the Untouchables; originally aboriginals.

By 600 BC, the Indo-Aryans had formed monarchies in the Ganga plain, surrounded by smaller tribes resisting the Brahmanic orthodoxy and its authoritarianism.

Within the monarchies, thinkers took to the asceticism which has characterized spiritual life in India. The Brahmans cannily countered this threat by absorbing the new ideas into their teachings. But the tribes were less amenable and so became the breeding ground for two new religions espousing non-violence: Jainism and Buddhism.

While the Aryans fought for control of the Ganga valley, new invaders appeared at India's frontiers: Cyrus, Emperor of Persia, crossed the Hindu Kush mountains into the Indus valley in 530 BC. While Brahman and Persian scholars exchanged ideas, the Indians copied the Persian coin system. Rock-inscriptions left by Emperor Darius probably inspired the pillar-edicts of Indian Emperor Ashoka in the 3rd century BC.

The spectacular invasion by Alexander the Great of Macedonia in 326 BC ended Persian presence, but apart from opening up trade with Asia Minor and the eastern Mediterranean, the Greeks left no lasting impact on India during the two-year campaign.

Alexander's dreams of a huge empire extending eastwards across the Ganga plain were blocked by mutinous troops fed up with upset stomachs, the harsh terrain and the tough Indian military opposition. He returned to Babylon, leaving a few governors on the frontier.

Ajanta's cave-temples provided refuge from flood and plague for Buddhist and Jain monks.

Ashoka's Empire

Meanwhile, in the Ganga valley power-struggle, Magadha emerged (modern Bihar) as the dominant kingdom. Its ruler, Chandragupta Maurya (321-297 BC), was also to become the founder of India's first imperial dynasty with Pataliputra, (modern Patna) as its capital – the world's largest city at the time.

Chandragupta extended his rule to the north-west with a rigorous campaign against the Greek forces of Seleucus Nikator. It ended in a profitable marriage alliance with the Greeks, but later Chandragupta turned to more sober thoughts: he converted to Jainism, and finally starved to death at the temple of Sravanabelagola.

His son Bindusara also liked to combine ambition with a taste for the good life and philosophy. He expanded the empire as far down as Mysore and stunned the western world by asking King Antiochus for Greek wine, figs and a sophist. The king was happy to send the wine and figs, but would not, however, consent to the brain-drain.

To control land and sea routes to the south, the Mauryas needed still to conquer the eastern kingdom of Kalinga (modern Orissa). The task was left to Bindusara's heir Ashoka, admired by Indians as their greatest ruler, perhaps for his special combination of tough authoritarianism and a high moral sense of righteousness.

Ashoka (269-232 BC) began by killing all his rivals before turning to conquer Kalinga in 260 BC. This left 100,000 dead, with even more dying from famine and disease, while 150,000 were taken captive.

This can be gathered from one of the famous inscriptions that he left as testimony to his reign on rocks and pillars everywhere. The inscription states how 'he of gentle visage and beloved of the gods', as he describes himself, was filled with remorse and converted to the non-violent teachings of Buddha, but its metaphysical implications seem to have interested him less than its moral example for his far-flung subjects to unite under him, in peace and fellowship.

To oversee this, Ashoka turned the Brahmanic concept of *dharma* (righteousness) into an instrument of public policy, enforced by the Officers of Righteousness he had appointed for this purpose.

The imperial administration for this demanded a huge bureaucracy, with superintendents, accountants and clerks overseeing commerce, forestry and, armoury, weights and measures, goldsmiths, prostitutes, ships, cows and horses, elephants, chariots and infantry.

Southern India remained independent, but Ashoka had his hands full with a large empire that now extended as far north as Kashmir and east to Bengal.

In the 50 years that followed Ashoka's death, Mauryan power went into decline. Agriculture was not productive enough to provide for the empire's expansion. Also, the unwieldy bureaucracy couldn't keep its loyalties straight with the too-rapid turnover in rulers vying for Ashoka's throne.

Invaders Galore

After the break-up of the Mauryan empire, new invaders appeared on the north-west frontier. The first to arrive were Bactrian Greeks left in the Afghan hills by Alexander's successors. They were welcomed for their erudite ideas on medicine, astronomy and astrology.

Joined by Iranian kings known as Pahlavas, the Greeks were over-run in the 1st century BC by bands of Scythian nomads known as the Shakas. They moved on into the Ganga valley when other nomads, the Yueh-chi from Central Asia, swept across the frontier.

Emerging victorious from the struggles between the Yueh-chi and the Shakas, King Kanishka of the Kushan established an empire from the northern half of India and into Central Asia. His reign was one of prosperity and made India a trade centre between east and west

Kanishka was a champion of the Mahayana (Great Vehicle) school that attributed for the first time a quasi-divinity to Buddha, and his active patronage of the arts led to the creation of the first bronze and stone sculptures of Buddha.

Buddhist and Jain merchants prospered with the new east-west trade and so were able to finance the magnificently sculpted cave-temples in the Deccan.

The arts also flourished in India during these early times. Madurai was the lively cultural centre for Dravidian artisttes: poets, actors, singers, musicians and also dancers who were precursors of the Hindu *devadasi* temple-prostitutes.

Gupta Glory

The Gupta dynasty, founded by the obscure Bihari landowner Chandra Gupta I, rose to power during the 4th century AD. Marriage-alliance and conquest allowed the Guptas to create an empire from Bengal to the Punjab and from Kashmir to the Deccan.

Samudra Gupta, the warrior of the clan, launched lightning raids through the jungles to snatch the gold of the south. The Guptas also capturing the western sea-ports and their trade with the Arabs. They turned their noses up at trade with the Romans, but China offered many bounties such as silk, musk and amber in exchange for India's spices, jewels and perfumes – as well as parakeets for the ladies' boudoirs and monkeys for their cooking-pots.

The Gupta empire began to crumble in the 5th century with the onslaught of the so-called White Huns. They were not clearly linked to Attila's Huns, but their harsh agenda of exterminating Buddhists does suggest an affinity. The White Huns seized the Punjab, Kashmir and a large portion of the western Ganga plain before being chased out again.

In the 7th century, one strong king, Harsha Vadhana, reigned for 40 years over northern India, and encouraged both Buddhist monks and Brahman priests to participate in philosophical discussions. Sages developed the strict disciplines of yoga and profound metaphysical speculations of Vedanta.

In southern India, power was shared by the plundering Pallavas in Kanchipuram and the Pandyas and Cholas vying for control of Thanjavur (Tanjore). The *bhakti* movement of the Tamils brought a new warmth to the hitherto rigid Brahmanic ritual of Hinduism. The temples of Mahabalipuram were a high point in southern architecture and it was the Pallavan artists who influenced and may have helped to build the temples at Angkor Wat in Cambodia and Borobudur in Java.

Islam Comes to India

Arab trade with India had long since whetted the appetites of the Moslems, and when Indian pirates plundered their ships off the coast of Sind in 711, it provoked the Governor of Chaldea (now Iraq) to send troops with 6,000 horses and 6,000 camels to conquer the Sind rajas and offer the alternative of converting to Islam or death.

When it was revealed to the Governor of Chalda that Hinduism was in fact a serious religion with too many faithful to treat in this way, another solution had to be found: Hindus, along with Parsis who had fled an earlier Moslem persecution in Persia, were given the privileged status of *dhimmi*, dues-paying non-believers.

For nearly 300 years, Islamic conquest in India was confined to this trading community in Sind, but in the 10th century tribesmen from Turkistan driven west by Chinese expansion, set up a state at Ghazni and began raids across the border to plunder Hindu temples.

South Indian carving inspired artists throughout the whole of South-east Asia.

Sweeping through the Punjab and Gujarat across to the western end of the Ganga valley, Mahmud of Ghazni (997-1030) used these raids more to finance his empire in Persia and Turkistan than to set up a permanent foothold in India.

Mahmud smashed the infidels' idols and destroyed their temples as he went, but was nonetheless cultured enough to use the booty to build a library, a museum and a splendid mosque when he got back to Ghazni. If Moslems saw him as a righteous militant, and Hindus as a brutal monster, neither denied him his title of 'Sword of Islam'. In order to understand his ambiguous image, compare him with Europe's heroic crusaders who went on the rampage at about the same time.

There was no concerted Indian response to the invasions because the various kingdoms were busy with wars of their own. The Rajput warrior-clans fought each other for control in what is now Rajasthan, the Kathiawar peninsula and as far east as Khajuraho. The Turco-Afghan invaders were regarded as a transient phenomenon that would either soon disappear or, just like others before them, be swallowed up by the great subcontinent.

A Sultan for Delhi

At the end of the 12th century, the Turks arrived: sultan Mohammed of Ghur and his Mameluke (slave) General Qutb-ud-din Aybak seized Ghazni in 1173 and invaded India with their huge forces. The Rajputs made a belated alliance and fought valiantly from one desert fortress to another, but their elephants could not match their opponents' fast horses and Afghan cavalry firing superior crossbows at the gallop. By 1193, the Turks were masters in Peshawar, Lahore and Delhi.

The sultan returned to Ghazni and, leaving Qutb-ud-din in charge, moved east to Bengal, destroying centres of Buddhism such as the University of Nalanda.

After his master's assassination in 1206, Qutb-ud-din proclaimed himself sultan of Delhi, head of India's first Islamic dynasty. The sultanate lasted 320 years, but the new sultan ruled only four years: he died in a fall from his pony.

After the shock of the invasion had passed, the Turks proved to be a shot in the arm for India.

The Persian language spoken at court enriched Indian literature and combined with the Sanskrit-based dialects of northern India to create Hindustani. Painting and architecture were infused with life, roads were paved and in the 14th century Delhi was pronounced by the Arab traveller Ibn Batuta to be the most magnificent city in the whole of the Moslem world.

Conversion to the Islamic faith was seen as a means of advancement, and those Rajputs who didn't take advantage of this offer were able to sharpen their martial skills in constant guerilla warfare.

The Turks adopted the Indian cuisine and costume as best suited to the climate, and a modified form of the Hindu caste-system. Highest were those of foreign extraction such as Turks, Arabs, Afghans and Persians, known as *ashraf*, that is 'honourable'. Then came upper-caste converts from Hinduism, the 'clean' castes of both merchants and artisans, and then the 'unclean' occupations of scavengers.

Qutb-ud-din celebrated his Delhi conquest by building a tower to survey the city.

29

It's worth noting that the first – and last – Moslem woman to rule in India was Qutb-ud-din's grand-daughter Raziyya. 'Wise, just and generous,' a contemporary Moslem historian said of her, 'but she was not born of the right sex and so all the virtues were worthless.' Three years of her wisdom, justice and generosity were all they could take before they murdered her.

What they seemed to want was a despot like one Ala-ud-din Khalji (1296-1316), who forced Mongol invaders back across the Afghan frontier and then moved through the peninsula to its southern tip.

Ala-ud-din's successors did not assert control of the territory. The south remained dominated by the Hindu kingdom of Vijayanagar for the next 250 years.

The Delhi sultanate under the Tughlaq dynasty could no longer hold its own in the north, and so Moslem kingdoms began to form in Bengal and the Deccan.

The end was hastened by a man who made other Moslem invaders seem like pussy cats: the Mongol Timur the Lame, the 'barbarous and bloody Tamburlaine'; he was later written about by Elizabethan playwright Christopher Marlowe.

On the grounds that the sultans were too soft, he cut through Delhi in 1398, slaughtering thousands of Hindus and carrying off thousands more as slaves. He left behind him famine and pestilence, with the Turks' Indian empire in splinters, passing into the hands of Afghan horse-breeders, the Lodi, who later succumbed to his descendants, the Mughals.

Down on the Malabar coast, the great Portuguese explorer Vasco da Gama landed in 1498, paving the way for his countrymen to form a settlement in Goa. The merchants wanted to divert trade away from the Arabs, fearing the enrichment of the North African Maghreb as a threat to Christian Europe.

With them came the Catholic missionaries who found the best subjects for their teachings among the low-caste Hindus. Around 1548 St. Francis Xavier began his mission among the pearl fishermen of Goa, before he set sail for Japan. To deal with the small communities of Jews and Nestorian Christian 'heretics', who had settled down on the Malabar coast in the mists of antiquity, the then Archbishop of Goa opened a local branch of the Holy Inquisition.

The merchants at first tried the soft sell, offering cloth, wine and necklaces for ivory and gold, but the traders of Calicut were insulted at being taken for 'natives' who could be bought with cheap hooch and glass baubles. The Portuguese turned to the harder sell of naval batteries, driving off a trading fleet in the year 1509 in order to control the Malabar coast. With hardly any women present in the colony, the Portuguese soldiers took Indian wives. Many Goans are descended from them or from converts who took the name of their Portuguese sponsors.

The Great Mughals

The new conquerors of northern India did not come uninvited. The Afghan governors of the Sind and the Punjab, and who were hoping for more autonomy than they had under the lofty sultan Ibrahim Lodi in Delhi, therefore called on Babur, the Tiger, King of Kabul.

Babur the Tiger, descendant of Timur the Lame and of Genghis Khan, accepted their welcome, but made no promises. With cannons, hitherto unknown in India, his men crushed sultan Ibrahim's 50,000 at Panipat, north of Delhi.

It was the morning of April 21, 1526, the beginning of the empire of the Mughals – the term used for descendants of Babur as distinct from those of Genghis Khan, who are referred to as 'Mongols' even though the term is etymologically the same.

Babur quickly captured Delhi and Agra, with resistance coming from the Rajputs, before he could conquer the Afghan chiefs in 1529. He died a year later.

His heir, Humayun, preferred opium and astrology to complex State affairs, and was driven out of India into Persia by General Sher Shah, who proved to be a much more able ruler. In five years, the General built new roads, created a royal postal service and set the pattern of Mughal administration for the next two centuries before dying in battle and leaving the throne to a number of inept successors and the return of Humayun.

Straightened out for a while, Humayun came back in 1555 with his Persian army to recapture the Punjab, Delhi and Agra, but the next year, his opium habit caused his death in a rather silly accident (see p. 67). The one clever thing he did was leave a son named Akbar.

Jalal-ud-din Mohammed Akbar (1556–1605) was a real emperor. Typical of his genius was the new religion he offered his subjects: the Divine Faith *(Din-Ilahi)* intended to satisfy orthodox Moslems and those who, just like himself and the Hindus. appreciated the idea of a semi-divine ruler.

Keen to win the allegiance of the Hindus, Akbar abolished most of the discriminatory taxes on non-Moslems, and recruited Rajputs for his army after marrying a daughter of Raja Bharmal of Amber, but did not flinch at massacring another Rajput's 8,000 soldiers.

Despite repeated efforts, Akbar could not extend his empire south. In 1565, the Moslem sultanates of the Deccan had taken the Hindu empire of Vijayanagar by means of slaughter, but they were not going to hand it all to Akbar.

Although illiterate, Akbar had enormous intellectual curiosity. He preferred Sufi mysticism to orthodox Islam, and held debates with Brahmans, and Jain monks, Parsi Zoroastrians, and Jesuits. The more orthodox Moslems were concerned that Islam was being abandoned and rebellions sprang up in Bengal, Bihar and the Punjab.

While Akbar was fighting in the Deccan in 1601, his son claimed the throne. Akbar rushed back to reassert his power but he died soon after, poisoned, it is rumoured, by his son. The new emperor called himself Jahangir, 'World Seizer', but once in power he lost interest in seizing the world and left affairs of state to his wife Nur Jahan.

Jahangir was more interested in writing poetry, drinking a great deal of wine and taking summer excursions up to Kashmir. In the capital at Agra, rich Persian culture dictated taste in dress and décor, manners and morals, enriched by the Hindu culture of the Rajputs in literature, cuisine and sexuality.

If the peasants were squeezed by taxes to pay for the luxury of Mughal court life, it was a boon for the country's artisans – goldsmiths, jewellers and weavers. In such an atmosphere, incidents of highway banditry increased and the district governors shared the rich booty in exchange for a pardon when the bandits were captured.

Humayun's tomb: religion was not his opium, but rather opium was his religion.

Jahangir was equally at home with Hindu ascetics and Jesuit missionaries. He was so polite to the latter that they reported to Rome he was ripe for conversion. In fact, he was just being polite.

His son Shahjahan became the biggest spender of all the Mughals. He lavished millions on palaces and mosques, blowing at least one million pounds sterling on gold and jewels for his Peacock Throne, but the imperial treasury allotted only 5,000 rupees a week for the plague and famine victims of 1631.

Of several hundred women in the emperor's harem, his only love was the now legendary Mumtaz-Mahal ('Exalted of the Palace'), by whom he had 14 children. She died in childbirth and Shahjahan built her the most famous memorial a man ever offered to the woman he loved: the Taj Mahal.

Shahjahan's son was Aurangzeb (1658–1707), who overthrew his father and imprisoned him in the Agra fort for the last years of his life. A pious Moslem, puritanical in both clothes and personal tastes, he banished music from the court and burned the portraits of princes as breaches of the Islamic taboo on craven images.

Gone, too, was any notion of religious tolerance. The Sikhs were slaughtered, the Hindu temples in both Varanasi and Mathura were destroyed, with the building of new temples was forbidden. Taxes on non-Moslems were brought back and Hindu merchants forced to pay double duties on their goods.

Aurangzeb streamlined the lax administration of his predecessors, but he almost bankrupted the realm with his campaigns to expand the empire down to the south and his battles against rebels in the north.

The most significant resistance came from Marathas, today's State of Maharashtra, around Bombay. They were led by the fighter Sivaji (1627-1680), bandit and bravest of military leaders, and an authentic Hindu folk-hero.

Starting out from Pune (Poona), Sivaji's Marathas fought off the Deccan sultans at Bijapur, and the Mughals at Purandar. Aurangzeb forced him finally to submit, but the humiliating reception he was given at court sent him back on the war-path again.

Sivaji then had himself crowned King of the Marathas and, to pay his soldiers, plundered the country all the way east to Madras.

The British Arrive

Meanwhile, by the middle of the 17th century, Dutch and British armed merchant-ships had broken through the Portuguese blockade to set up their East India Companies on both coasts.

Arriving in 1608, the British took five years to get their foot in the Indian door, at the western port of Surat, north of Bombay.

The Company destroyed the Portuguese fleet and took over the protection of the Moslem pilgrimage ships to Mecca, but there were no hard feelings; the Portuguese made a gift of Bombay to King Charles II in 1661 as part of the dowry of Catherine of Braganza. The Indians were not consulted.

The Company erected its east coast installations in the year 1642 just down the road from the Dutch, at Mandaraz, pronounced 'Madras' by the British. Further north, the British gradually gained the upper hand over its rivals, now including the French, for the Bengali trade that was to create Calcutta.

The Mughal empire had five rulers in 12 years after Aurangzeb died. Bihar, Bengal and Rajputana all went separate ways. The Sikhs reacted violently to persecution,

and the Marathas spread to Orissa, after which, in the year 1739, Nadir Shah of Persia invaded and carried off the Peacock Throne (broken up after his assassination).

Meanwhile, the British under clerk-turned-soldier Robert Clive, won a long campaign against the French for Madras.

Fearing the Europeans would start carving up Bengal, the nawab (Moslem prince) Siraj-ud-daula set up an attack on the British settlement in Calcutta on the hot day of June 20, 1756. Those who did not flee to sea were thrown into Fort William's prison, already known as the Black Hole.

It's still being debated whether 123 suffocated and 23 survived or 'only' 43 died with 21 survivors, but it was enough for Clive to crush Siraj-ud-daula at the Battle of Plassey. Clive became governor and placed his own nawab on the throne, in exchange for £500,000 for himself and the Company. He tyen annexed about 2,330 sq km (900 sq miles) of land due south of Calcutta to provide rents for the British settlement and to guarantee himself an income of £30,000 per year for life. The rise of the British Empire in India had begun.

Installing the Raj

The arrival of Indian merchants, including Jains, Parsis and Jews, turned many Bombay, Madras and Calcutta into large cities and the Company discovered a knack for large-scale administration. A high sense of integrity took the place of what Clive called the 'fighting, chicanery, intrigues, politics and Lord knows what'.

In return for fixed payments to the emporer, the Company officials collected revenue, and with a well-paid civil service, Clive's successors, Warren Hastings and Lord Cornwallis, avoided the collectors padding their salaries with private deals. With the new title of Governor-General, Hastings and then Cornwallis were responsible to the British government rather than the Company. Britain began taking India more seriously.

But this new high-mindedness had in it the seeds of what was to be future discontent. Indians were removed from key positions in the administration because Cornwallis considered them not yet up to the stricter ethical standards that were being introduced. It took a long time for them to be readmitted to positions of responsibility.

Clive's example in Calcutta set the pattern for territorial control around the country. In the south, Tipu Sultan of Mysore remained a menace to Madras until Governor-General Arthur Wellesley, future Duke of Wellington, defeated him.

Wellesley then turned on the Marathas, whose clans controlled the puppet Mughal emperor in Delhi and much of central India. A few brilliant victories gained for Britain control of Orissa and other territories, but London decided all that energy would be best directed at Napoleon and called him home.

When territory wasn't acquired by conquest – Sind from Baluchi princes, Punjab and Kashmir from the Sikhs, Maharashtra and Delhi from the Marathas or Assam from Burma – the British annexed it by so-called Principles of Lapse and Paramountcy. If a ruler died without direct heir, his state 'lapsed' into British hands. If, after repeated warnings, a State was judged guilty of misgovernment, it was simply annexed by the Paramount Power – the British.

Schools and colleges became established. Calcutta became the centre of a vigorous free press and the intellectual capital of India.

During 1834, regional rupees of differing value were minted with the portrait of the Mughal emperor. Then a national rupee of unitary value was issued, with the face of the king of England. In running the empire well, the British installed railways and better roads, the telegraph and stamp-post. Indians also saw the other side of the Industrial Revolution as their cotton left for Manchester to come back as cloth cheaper than their own.

Good men auch as Governor-General William Bentinck worked with missionaries and reformers such as Brahman Ram Mohan Roy to legislate against the practice of widows becoming *sati* by climbing onto their husband's funeral pyre. Other campaigns were launched against female infanticide, slavery, and the bands of Thugs (devotees of Kali) ranging the countryside.

Although some Indians assimilated the language and behaviour of the British, for most they were offensively aloof. The Indians had known other conquerors, but at least they had been able to gain a sense of them as human beings. The British Raj, though, was firmly entrenched in clubs, and remained resolutely separate.

Mutiny and Reform

The cause of the Mutiny of 1857 was symptomatic of British insensitivity. Indian troops were trained to bite the cartridges before loading their rifles, but some were greased with animal fat and the Indians felt they were ingesting either fat from the cow, sacred to the Hindus, or lard from the pig, abomination to the Moslems. As they had suffered slights of either incomprehension or contempt for their religious customs before, they simply could not believed it was not deliberate, and mutiny broke out at Meerut, 40 km (25 miles) north of Delhi.

The cartridge blunder became a pretext for avenging other grievances, with troops rallying around the rulers dispossessed by Lapse or Paramountcy. The mutineers then invaded Delhi, Kanpur (Cawnpore) and Lucknow, looting treasuries, breaking open jails and killing British men, women and children.

The British retaliated with equal savagery against the mutineers as well as against civilians in the country through which the relief columns passed. Finally, the last of the proud Mughals, the Emperor Bahadur Shah, was condemned to exile in Burma.

Nothing could more aptly epitomize the Mutiny's good and bad results, from an Indian point of view, than the name given to the legislation that was to follow: the 1858 Act for Better Government of India. The British evidently saw the need to improve things for the Indians, but also decided to tighten their imperial hold.

The East India Company was replaced by a Government with a Viceroy answering to a Secretary of State for India in London. The bureaucracy was to be streamlined, the army reorganized to raise the ratio of British to Indians.

Indian education was greatly expanded, though less successfully in rural areas where people thought

it better to be a good peasant than a bad clerk. Queen Victoria, who in the year 1876 would add the title Empress of India to her roll of honour, proclaimed that the Indian Civil Service would be open to 'our subjects of whatever race and creed'. Not a lot of Indians could afford the trip to Britain to take the examination.

Meanwhile, lawyers were at a premium – Indians love litigation and it was ideal training for future politicians – and politics had been clandestine, because it was so often fatal to express an opinion on the wrong, i.e. losing, side. Now open political debate flourished, especially in Calcutta where Karl Marx was much appreciated.

Indian entrepreneurs developed their own cotton mills in Bombay, Ahmedabad, Kanpur and Madras, but the new tea gardens were a strictly British affair. Indian agricultural products soon found new markets in Europe when the Suez Canal was opened in 1869.

In the arts, the Architecture was often of the work of engineers and huge sculptures were ordered from Victorian Britain rather than from local artists. The bright spot was the Archaeological Survey of 1871 to preserve ancient monuments. British soldiers hunting tigers in the jungle were finding temples and palaces the Indians no longer knew existed.

East meets West in the Mughal Gothic architecture of Bombay's Victoria Terminus.

Fighting for Self-Rule

The Indian National Congress, the country's first political party, held its inaugural meeting in Bombay in 1885. As a group of liberal Hindu and Parsi intellectuals, supported by a few progressive British, it was more national in purpose than in its representation. Lacking connection with the peasants, it was also distrusted by conservative landlords and by most Moslems. The goal of *swaraj* ('self-rule'), proclaimed in 1906, was seen by a moderate Left Centre group as government within the British Empire and by a breakaway revolutionary Extreme Left group as complete independence.

After years of subservience to the West, artists returned to Indian themes in their literature, theatre and music. Indians applauded the decision of Lord Ripon to allow Indian magistrates to try British defendants in criminal cases, but attempts at social reform such as protecting child-brides against rape by their husbands were fought by traditionalist Hindus from Calcutta and Pune with cries of 'religion in danger'. Self assertion reigned again: after years of peace, hostilities broke out between the Hindus and the Moslems.

In Maharashtra, a cult grew up around the Maratha leader Sivaji (see pp. 34-35) against the British and also the Moslems whom Sivaji had fought all his life. Fundamentalists took to the streets to protest against the Moslem slaughter of cows. There was a movement to convert Moslems and Christians back to the 'national' religion. The Moslems tried to purify the Islamic practice of the Hindu rituals which had accrued over the years.

The caste-system was affected by this new spirit. Untouchables pressed for better treatment, but their cause was not helped by the activism of American missionaries and the Salvation Army who gave other castes a good excuse to resist 'foreign interference'.

Dynamic Lord Curzon, viceroy from 1899 to 1905, was driven by a lofty imperial vision of the British role in India. His grandiose life in the viceregal residence in Calcutta or palace in Simla was worthy of the Mughal emperors.

Highly active in excavating and restoring the temples and palaces, Curzon also did more than any of his predecessors, adding 9,000 km (5,500 miles) of new railway lines, working to modernize farming with an agricultural research institute, and making the irrigation a model for Asia and Africa. The Indians, however, resented his refusal to consult them, and rioted over an ill-considered partition of Bengal.

In 1911, King George V became the first British monarch to visit India. He celebrated the fact by announcing that the capital would be moved from Calcutta to a whole new city to be built in Delhi. The Royal architects Edwin Lutyens and Herbert Baker created a monumental New Delhi with triumphal arch, palace, gigantic government buildings and sweeping avenues radiating from circles (for easy riot control) – the stuff of an empire meant to last forever.

Without giving up demands for self-determination, India fought at Britain's side in World War I, and more than one Prussian general blinked at Rajput and Sikh princes leading an Indian infantry through the trenches of France.

In 1917 self-determination in India seemed nearer when London announced its plan for 'the progressive realization of responsible government in India as an integral part of the (British) Empire.' The British were not letting go, but a new Government of India Act two years later promised Indians real executive power at the head of provincial ministries for education, public works, health and agriculture. The moderate Indians were delighted, but revolutionaries saw it as a foot in the door, while many British officials retired rather than serve under Indian ministers.

There were riots over Bengal's partition that led to new laws for political trials without jury and also internment without trial. Popular protest in the big cities in 1919 at first took the non-violent form of a *hartal*, an Indian 'strike' called when the soul was shocked by an injustice. This idea came from the new leader Mohandas Karamchand Gandhi, dubbed Mahatma – which means 'Great Soul' – by the Indian poet Rabindranath Tagore.

Ghandi returned in 1915 after working as a lawyer defending the rights of the Indian community in South Africa. The moral strength of his non-violent philosophy was immediately tested in the Punjab, where the *hartal* erupted into riots. In Amritsar, the troops of General Reginald Dyer fired on a prohibited mass meeting, leaving 379 dead and over 1,200 wounded.

As a result, Gradualist reform became discredited and civil unrest a feature of everyday life.

Declaring that 'cooperation in any form with this satanic government is sinful', Ghandi advocated the boycott of elections and the withdrawal of people from government office. Moderates held on, but the election boycott was at least 33 percent successful.

Abandoning European dress for his now legendary white cotton *dhoti* (loin-cloth) and shawl and drawing spiritual guidance from all the great religions of India, Ghandi had become the simple but powerful symbol of India. He supported the Untouchables and defended the rights of village artisans and peasants, but his non-violent movement could not stop the escalating riots among the religious communities.

Worried by the spread of his civil disobedience movement, the British jailed Gandhi in 1922 for two years. In jail at the same time, for 'incitement to rebellion', was Congress Party militant Jawaharlal Nehru, who was British-educated but a Brahman intellectual as his honorary title of Pandit suggested. He was the Mahatma's favourite to lead India to independence.

Independence with Partition

The British began to see India's independence as inevitable, however only a few seemed to understand the vital role of the religious groups. Britain prepared a parliamentary democracy with majority rule, but the majority were Hindus – and Hindus, Moslems and Sikhs had been killing each other in war for many centuries.

Nehru's Congress Party, largely Hindu with a socialist leadership, wanted a parliamentary democracy. To provide a counterweight, British legislation reserved parliamentary seats for religious minorities, but the Punjab and Bengal had such a complicated mixture of Hindus, Moslems and Sikhs that it was not possible to avoid fights over how separate constituencies were to be formed. The seeds of future trouble were sown.

The legislation on reserving seats gave the Moslems the basis for an alternative against an India in which they were only a quarter of the population: Partition. In 1930, the poet Muhammad Iqbal proposed a separate Moslem homeland in the north-west of India. A small group of Indian Moslems at Cambridge came up with the name Pakistan, using the initials of the Punjab, Afghania (NW Frontier Province), Kashmir and Sind (at the same time producing the word *pak*, meaning 'pure') and adding 'stan', the Persian suffix for the word 'country'. The Moslem campaign for Partition was led by London-trained Bombay lawyer, Muhammad Ali Jinnah.

Meanwhile, Gandhi vehemently opposed any dismemberment of the country, and tried to keep people going with fasts to uphold the spirit of love, and by focussing on the common adversary: the British.

Gandhi led a march to the sea to protest the British salt tax.

Advocating civil disobedience, he led his famous Salt March to the sea, to scoop up salt and circumvent the hated British salt tax. This put more than 60,000 in jail.

Against this militancy, World War II did not elicit the solidarity of the first. Indians courageously fought alongside the British troops, in Burma, the Middle East and Europe, but Gandhi saw the British as a provocation for Japanese invasion and was jailed yet again, for launching a 'Quit India' campaign in the year 1942. The anti-British extremists even saw the Japanese as an Asian liberator.

Winston Churchill didn't want any Indian independence and so it was probably as well for India that he was defeated by Attlee's Labour Party in 1945.

With riots growing ever more bloody in Bengal, Bihar and the Punjab, India's last viceroy, Lord Mountbatten, kept a mandate to make the British departure as quick and as smooth as possible. Quick it was – six months after his arrival – but not smooth.

Midnight, August 14-15, in the year 1947, was a moment, in the words of Prime Minister Nehru, 'when we step out from the old to the new, when an age ends, and when the soul of a nation, long suppressed, finds utterance.'

Nehru got his Independence and Jinnah his Partition – a Pakistan in which its eastern Bengali portion was to break away 24 years later to become Bangladesh.

Bloodshed began as soon as the Partition boundaries were set. In east (Indian) Punjab, Hindus and Sikhs massacred Moslems, in west (Pakistani) Punjab, the Moslems massacred Sikhs and Hindus. This was followed by a mass exodus of millions from one country to the other but the convoys often ended in slaughter. Delhi itself was torn apart by communal rampages. The overall death toll came to at least 500,000 people.

Mahatma Gandhi immediately rushed from Calcutta to Delhi to defend Moslems against further slaughter. In January of the year 1948, he fasted for peace in the capital city in order to force the Indian government to pay Pakistan the monies due in the Partition's division of assets. A Hindu fanatic, enraged by what he felt was an indifferent defence of the Moslem interests, assassinated Gandhi in a prayer meeting on January 30.

India Today

Sensitive and sophisticated, Pandit Nehru was also the strongest ruler India had known since the great Mughals and, like them, he created a powerful dynasty. Rejecting his mentor Gandhi's faith in a village-based democracy, Nehru worked to make India a fully industrialized society on the basis of democratic socialism. Established industries had their taxes raised but were not nationalized. Companies that were foreign had to accept Indian financial participation and management.

He appropriated for the State much of the personal fortunes of the princes, but found it harder to curtail the power of land-owners who had extensive contacts with the more conservative elements in his Congress Party.

Kashmir stayed an unresolved problem of Partition. The Moslem majority in the Vale of Kashmir and Gilgit made it part of Pakistan, but the greater patrt of the eastern region around Jammu was Hindu, as was the maharaja. Backed by Pakistan Pathan tribesmen invaded Kashmir in 1947 to force the issue, but were soon repulsed by Indian troops flown in when the maharaja hastily acceded to India.

Kashmir was divided between both India and Pakistan, pending a plebiscite – which has never been held. An invasion by Pakistan in 1965 was aborted and has left the issue distinctly moot.

Applying the principle of geographical integrity, Nehru regained French Pondicherry by negotiation after Independence and Portuguese Goa by force in 1961. He was less successful in fighting China over territory on Tibetan frontier.

Egalitarian and agnostic, Nehru passed laws against the injustice of the caste-system – child marriage, and the treatment of women in Hindu households – but century old customs die hard: before his death in 1964, he asked that his ashes be scattered in the Yamuna river at Delhi and the Ganga at Allahabad, and without ritual. The mourning crowds, though, ignored his last wishes, uttering prayers and crying: 'Panditji has become immortal.'

Coming to power in the year 1966 after the brief ministry of Lal Bahadur Shastri, Indira Gandhi proved strong enough in her own right for people to stop describing her as Nehru's daughter or as 'not related to Mahatma Gandhi'.

In fact, she learned much from both, the knack for power-politics of the one and the massive popular appeal of the other. She accelerated industrialization, in particular the nuclear power industry, including a first atomic explosion in the desert in 1974. Her proudest achievement though was the Green Revolution which modernized wheat and rice farming to give India, for the first time in its history, self-sufficiency in food production. Old entrenched conservatism hampered her birth-control programmes to check the rocketing population growth.

Her tendency to tough authori-tarianism was highlighted during the repressive state of emergency she declared in 1975, describing

it as 'disciplined democracy', and when she ordered mass arrests of those opposition leaders who had charged her and her party with malpractice and corruption.

The electorate punished her in 1977 with three years in the wilderness, then brought her back with a huge majority, but her second term was beset with the problems of

regional unrest, most notably in Assam in the north-eastern region of the country, where local massacres left 3,000 dead, and in the Punjab where Sikh militants staged violent demonstrations for greater autonomy and even independence. It was her order to the Indian Army in 1984 to attack armed militants in the Sikhs' sacred Golden Temple in Amritsar, resulting in 800 dead, that led to her assassination in Delhi five months later by two Sikh members of her security guards. Hindus then went on the rampage through Sikh communities with the result that a round of communal violence ensured.

Those politicians who were to follow her, including also her son, Rajiv Gandhi, were beset with the many and complex problems of corruption and communal conflict. In the meantime, India continues to modernize its industry, and to face the challenges of an ever growing population that threatens to outnumber even that of China by the beginning of the next century.

Modern India looms behind the age-old trade of busy Bombay fishermen.

HISTORICAL LANDMARKS

Prehistory ca. 30,000-1500 BC		Stone Age peoples settle in India. First farmers in Baluchistan.
First Civilization 2300-1700 BC		Indus River valley civilization.
Indo-Aryan Migration 1500-530 BC	1500 530	Indo-Aryans enter India. Buddhism founded.
Persians and Greeks 530-326 BC	530 326	Persians invade Indus valley. Alexander crosses Indus into Punjab.
Mauryan Empire 321-185 BC	321 269-232	Chandragupta Maurya founds first Indian empire. Reign of Emperor Ashoka.
Nomad Invasions 185 BC-300 AD	100 BC. 98 AD	Scythians and Yueh-chi invade. Kushan empire.
Gupta Empire 320-495 AD	320	Chandra Gupta founds empire enriched by trade with China.
Islam in India 711-1193	711 1001-1030	Arabs invade Sind. Mahmud of Ghazni plunders Punjab, Gujarat and Ganga valley.
Turco-Afghan Domination 1193-1526	1193 1336 1398	Turco-Afghan forces conquer Delhi, and install sultanate. Foundation of Hindu kingdom of Vijayanagar in south. Timur the Lame (Tamberlaine) sacks Delhi.
Mughal Empire 1526-1756	1526 1556-1605 1605 1612 1642	Mughal empire begins. Reign of Emperor Akbar. Jahangir seizes Mughal throne. English merchants start trade in Surat (near modern Bombay). English establish East India Company in Madras.

	1646-1680	Sivaji leads Hindu Marathas against Mughals.
	1698	East India Company establishes settlement at Calcutta.
Rise of British Empire 1756-1858	1757	Battle of Plassey secures English hold on Bengal.
	1799	Defeat of Tipu Sultan.
	1803	British take Delhi.
	1849	Sikhs defeated, cede Punjab.
	1857	Indian Mutiny.
	1858	Last Mughal emperor exiled to Burma.
Road to Independence 1858-1947	1858	Better Government of India Act.
	1885	Indian National Congress founded.
	1911	George V first monarch to visit India. New Delhi nominated capital.
	1919	British troops kill 379 at Amritsar.
	1930	Gandhi's Salt March.
	1947	Independence for India and Pakistan.
India Today 1947-	1947-64	Jawaharlal Nehru Prime Minister.
	1948	Mahatma Gandhi assassinated.
	1962	War with China.
	1965	Pakistani invasion of Kashmir repelled.
	1966-77	Indira Gandhi's first term.
	1974	Experimental atomic explosion in Rajasthan desert.
	1984	Indian Army storms Sikh Temple. Indira Gandhi assassinated.
	1990	Communal violence in Kashmir.
	1991	Rajiv Ghandi assassinated.

RELIGIONS OF INDIA

Although the constitution of today describes India as a secular State, religion still plays a vital part in everyday life in its streets as well as in the architecture, sculpture and painting of its great monuments. A little background information to the major forms of faith may help

Hinduism

If Hinduism is more or less India's national cult, it's because it offers something for everyone: mysticism and metaphysics for scholars, ceremony for ordinary people, austerity sensuality, tranquillity and frenzy.

Building on the ancient cults and Vedic teachings of the Indo-Aryans, Hinduism began to take its present form in the 4th century AD under considerable pressure for a more 'accessible' religion. Popular devotional worship, with its appeal to the common people, replaced the sacrifices practised exclusively by the Brahmans.

It is said there are 330 million gods in the Hindu pantheon, but they might be seen as 330 million facets of a single divinity. The three most important gods are Brahma, Vishnu and Shiva, which are often presented to Westerners as a trinity, though it is not really comparable to the Christian concept.

The 'big three' are by no means accorded equal status. Vishnu, the preserver, is regarded by his worshippers as a god from whose navel a lotus grew bearing Brahma and whose only task it was to create the world. Vishnu, a four-armed god with mace, conch, discus and lotus, has many incarnations, of which the most famous is Krishna, who appears as conquering hero, flute-playing lover or mischievous baby. Vishnu's wife Lakshmi is goddess of good fortune.

Shiva is the dancing destroyer-god, wearing a garland of skulls and with snakes around both neck and arms. As the god of time and ascetics, he decides the fate of the world. As Lord of beasts and king of dance, Shiva is as passionate as Vishnu is serene. Just in case you think you have got it all clear in your mind, remember that Vishnu destroys by not preserving and Shiva preserves through the renewal arising from destruction.

No penetrating the inner world of a Hindu yogi.

By the 19th century, reformers such as the Bengali Brahman Ram Mohan Roy tried to rid Hinduism of idolatry and primitive practices. The self-immolation of widows, known as *sati* – a widow becomes *sati*, a 'virtuous woman', by climbing onto her husband's funeral pyre – has disappeared, but the monkey-god Hanuman and elephant-headed Ganesh are still idolised, and nobody will dare to deny the sanctity of the cow and her products: milk, curd, butter, urine and dung.

Hindu ethics say that the path to salvation has three principles: righteousness, prosperity honestly achieved and, not least, pleasure.

At the centre of the confrontation with the harsh reality of daily life is the concept of *karma*, that is 'work' or 'deed', and implying that the sum total of a one's acts in a previous life will determine one's present station in life. It promises a better reincarnation.

While this teaching has served to sustain the rigid hierarchy of the caste-system (see p. 21), it is not so 'fatalistic' as some would have it. The Hindus say we cannot escape our *karma* but that with good judgment and foresight, we can use it to our advantage.

Islam

Islam is not an Indian religion and that has been its problem. After a contact almost as old as Islam itself, a peaceful coexistence with Hinduism seems hard to achieve.

It's hard to imagine anything more hostile to all idolatry, fierce in its uncompromising monotheism, and opposed to the caste-system. When *sufi* mystics or the emperor Akbar tried to create a synthesis between the two faiths, the orthodox on both sides resisted.

Hindu conversions to Islamic faith were more often performed out of hope of social advancement under a Moslem government than out of conviction, but Moslems in India today are mostly descendants of those converts and as fervent as their brethren in Pakistan or the Middle East.

They also have divisions into Sunnites (adherents of the Sunna law expounded by Mohammed's own words and deeds) and Shiites (followers of those interpretations proposed by Mohammed's cousin Ali). Every day, the devout face Mecca, bow their foreheads to the ground and proclaim: 'There is no god but God; and Mohammed is His Prophet.'

Amritsar's Golden Temple plays the role of shrine and fortress for beleaguered Sikhs.

Sikhism

The one attempt to create a strong religion out of Hinduism and Islam is that of the Sikhs ('disciples').

Nanak, their *guru* (teacher), was born a Hindu in 1469 and reared on the egalitarian principles of Islam. He opposed idolatry and the caste-system (subsequently too strong to resist). From Islam he took the idea of one God, but refused any such specific conception as Allah.

He saw God's manifestation, like Hinduism, as being everywhere in the world He created.

Nanak's teachings were written in the *Adi Granth*, which acquired for Sikhs the sanctity of the Koran. According to this faith, alcohol and tobacco are forbidden.

The militancy of the Sikhs came about only as Nanak's successors got embroiled in politics and with dire results for the Sikhs when their leaders challenged the Mughals. After the execution of Guru Tegh Bahadur, his son, Guru Gobind Singh, exalted the faithful to be ever ready for armed defence.

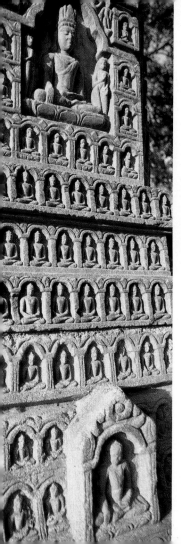

They were all took the surname Singh, meaning 'Lion' (all Sikhs are named Singh, but not all Singhs are Sikhs), and wore a turban and the five K's: *kesha* (uncut hair and beard), *kanga* (comb for their hair), *kara* (steel bracelet), *kachha* (soldier's shorts) and *kirpan* (dagger). Their distinctive appearance made them highly visible and imposed an unflinching courage.

Buddhism

Buddhism was founded over 2,500 years ago in reaction to Brahmanic orthodoxy and practically vanished as an organized religion from the Indian scene by persecution and absorption into the Hindu mainstream. It continues, however, to exert influence on India's spiritual and artistic life to the present day.

Buddha's own life explains his teachings but the truth is buried in both legend and historical fact: he was born Siddhartha Gautama in a grove of sal trees at Lumbini (just across the Nepalese border) around the year 566 BC. His mother, who was queen of the Sakyas, is said to have conceived him after dreaming that a magnificent white elephant holding a lotus flower in his trunk had entered her side.

Siddhartha grew up in princely luxury, but when he was taken out one day to the edge of the royal parks, he saw the poor, the sick and the aged. Then he saw a religious beggar who seemed serene, and he realized the path his life must take. Abandoning his riches, he went

Sikkim's Tibetan monks.

off into the kingdoms of the Ganga valley. For six years he begged for his food, learned to meditate and practised severe self-mortification, but still felt no nearer to understanding life's suffering. Then, aged 35, sitting under a tree at the place now known as Bodh Gaya (south of Patna), he vowed to stay there until his goal was achieved.

For 49 days he resisted demons and temptresses, and became truly Enlightened – Buddha as he is called today. He preached his new wisdom at Sarnath (near Varanasi) and with ever more disciples went out to spread his word. Buddha himself converted ruthless bandits and whole armies from the path of violence. In Kushinagar, between Bodh Gaya and his birthplace, he died aged 80, of dysentery, it is said, from eating pork.

Preaching that suffering came from the pursuit of personal desire, Buddha had advocated the Middle Way of the Eightfold Path: right views, right resolve, right speech and right conduct, right livelihood, right effort, right re-collection and right meditation. Only thus could the enlightenment of Nirvana be achieved.

This original doctrine without any sense of Buddha's divinity was embraced by the Hinayana (Lesser Vehicle) school which spread to Sri Lanka, Burma and Thailand, as well as Cambodia and Laos. The Mahayana (Great Vehicle) school added the concept of Bodhisattva as divine saviour, and was then the most dominant form of Buddhism, spreading to China and Japan.

After centuries of almost total eclipse, Buddhism has today been able to achieve a revival offering its egalitarian philosophy to Hindu Untouchables.

Jainism

As old as Buddhism, Jainism has made its mark with its concept of *ahimsa* (non-violence) and is much more pacifist than its name, which means religion of the conquerors.

Vardhamana Mahavira was its founder. He was born in 540 BC in Bihar and, like Buddha, was the son of a chief. He, too, abandoned riches to become an ascetic. But Mahavira (the Great Hero) pursued self-mortification to the end of his life, stripping off his clothes to take his word naked from kingdom to kingdom. He died of self-inflicted starvation at the age of 72 in Para, near Rajgir. His followers were later to divide into the *Digambaras* ('space-clad', i.e. naked) and the *Svetambaras* ('white-clad') you see today.

The religion, in which Mahavira is seen as the manifestation of 24 *Tirthankaras* (teachers), attributes souls to all living creatures, as well as other natural objects. Agriculture was therefore abandoned for

its destruction of plant and animal life. The doctrines survive in vegetarianism, with Jain monks carrying dusters to sweep insects away from where they tread and wear a gauze veil over their mouth to avoid breathing in flies.

Jainism never spread beyond India and claims 2 million followers, including many businessmen

Jain non-violence protects the life of even the humblest fly.

in Gujarat and the Deccan, with a few in Bengal. It had considerable influence on Mahatma Gandhi's non-violent movement, who used its fasting-unto-death as a potent moral and political weapon.

Parsis, Jews and Christians

The Parsis, as their name suggests, originate from ancient Persia and are today form only a minute community in the world of religions, with barely 100,000 living in India, mostly in and around the city of Bombay. They have been and are still enormously influential in this country's economic life, and have often served as all-important go-betweens in the often immensely difficult relations between Hindus and Moslems, India and Pakistan.

Their religion dates as far back to the 7th century BC, when their prophet Zoroaster contrasted his peaceful and sedentary People of Righteousness with the polytheistic nomadic People of Evil. His was an attitude that probably determined not only their general ethics but also their occupational destiny as highly sophisticated businessmen.

The Parsis base their elaborate code of ethics on the concept of a constant struggle existing between the forces of creation – that is light and good – and those of darkness and evil. It's teachings lays great emphasis on the very purity of the world's natural elements, fire, earth and water. So, for instance, to avoid polluting the elements, they do not bury or cremate their dead but lay them exposed and naked on their famous Towers of Silence, for the vultures to devour.

India's Jewish and Christian communities are ancient indeed. Some texts claim that the first Jews arrived in India at the time of the Babylonian exile, in 587 BC, others bring them to Cranganur, on the Malabar coast, in AD 72 – it was about this time that the disciple Thomas is thought to have brought his Christian mission to India. The oldest Jewish community still in existence is situated down the coast at Cochin (see p. 177), dating back at least to the 4th century AD. Some others, less orthodox, can be found in Bombay, but most emigrated to Israel when it was founded in the year 1948.

The earliest Christians other than St. Thomas (see p. 188), were the so-called Nestorian 'heretics' of the Syrian Orthodox Church, also living on the Malabar coast since the first centuries of the Christian era. Modern Christians are mainly Catholic living in Goa, and elsewhere you will find all the British variations on Protestantism, each with a certain inescapable Hindu tinge to them.

WHERE TO GO

Where, indeed? This subcontinent is so rich and varied, that the choice of what to see on a first visit can be daunting. Don't even *think* of 'doing' India the way people 'do' Europe.

With some judicious selection from among the places we suggest, you can most certainly get a pretty good feel for the country in the four weeks that most people devote to a first trip.

With a distinct taste for improvisation and a horror of schedules and detailed itineraries, you must accept from the outset, if your time is limited, that travelling around India will demand a certain amount of *planning*.

Remember: there are over 844 million Indians out there and a lot of them will be on the move at the same time as you, competing for plane seats and hotel rooms. So you will need to make at least some advance reservations for hotels in principal cities and especially for your major plane or train journeys. That can still leave you plenty of scope for getting off the beaten track and staying overnight in new and unexpected places.

Putting Together an Itinerary

We have divided the country into five regions – north, west, centre, east and south.

In each of the regions, you'll find a city like Delhi, Bombay or Madras which you can use as a starting point, and which would also be the best place for phoning home and making other practical arrangements. Equally important: each area includes a place where, in hallowed and sensible military phrasing, you can go for rest and recreation. In this case, you'll find a beach resort, nature reserve or one of the old hill-stations of the British Raj, each being ideal for a change of pace or climate. It's easy to overdose on the many temples, palaces and museums in India. They are worth your attention, but take plenty of time to relax too – you'll be surprised at how much more you can see and appreciate.

If your budget allows you to fly around the country, you can create a 'smorgasbord' of places to see in each region, since you will not be able to do all of them exhaustively. In any case, we recommend that you choose from at least two of them, ideally three, when planning your 'menu'.

PRACTICAL HINTS

The Tourist Information Offices can be very helpful. You will find their guides are much more reliable than those outside the temples or palaces, but one word of warning: tour guides will give contradictory explanations about the significance of statues as well as many different versions of legend and historical 'fact'. It would be easy to dismiss them as being nonsense, but you'll understand India better if you can appreciate that these explanations, at least in religious matters, may all in their own way be *true*. When it comes to ideas, there is no more tolerant land on earth.

Practical Hints

The Berlitz-Info section at the back of the book gives you details on how to handle the practical side of your trip. But it's worth keeping a few points in mind right now, when deciding where you're going in the time you have available.

The climate in India (see p. 223) imposes its own imperatives and restrictions on your itinerary.

Irrigation channels will bring desperately needed water to the parched earth.

Visit the Fort at Agra in style, in a maharaja's Palace on Wheels.

Kashmir is simply impractical in December, Delhi unbearably hot in June, and trains uncertain in the monsoon. Think of three seasons: *cool, hot,* and *wet,* emphasized here because they take on a particular meaning in the Indian context.

From October to March, *cool* – except in the northern hills and mountains, where it's bitterly cold – means pleasantly warm by day, fresh enough for a sweater in the evening until it starts hotting up by mid-February. The ideal season for seeing most of India.

From April to June, *hot,* is hot as most people only rarely experience it. The cities and plains in this

> **Like a Maharaja**
> *From the beginning of October to the end of March, Indian Railways organize one-week tours of Rajasthan (plus Agra and Delhi) on a train they call* Palace on Wheels, *reproducing the luxury once enjoyed only by maharajas.*
>
> *The train takes you from Delhi on to Jaipur, Udaipur, Jaisalmer, Jodhpur, Bharatpur, Agra and back to Delhi, with boat-cruises and rides on camels and proud elephants on the way. Book in advance from your travel agency before you leave home. It's not cheap, but then, that's what makes you feel like a maharaja.*

season are definitely a bad bet, but the hill-stations and Kashmir will be at their best.

From mid-June to September, *wet* means monsoon wet, not all day every day, but still torrential rains often enough to make travel uncertain and the mosquitoes and other bugs a real nuisance, but the country is at its most green and the temples, especially the Taj Mahal, take on a glistening beauty. The wet season is the best time of the year for a visit to Kashmir, which has no monsoon.

With regard to your health (see also p. 228), two attitudes herald a miserable time: carelessness and hypochondria. Don't exaggerate in either direction. Take elementary precautions by sticking to bottled drinks and freshly cooked food, and you won't have any serious stomach problems. An occasional touch of Delhi belly is unavoidable when you're not used to the spicy food, but nothing to worry about.

Take it easy, drink lots of liquids, and it'll pass. If you are on a short trip, you may need to take a quick-acting remedy to keep you on your feet, but if you load up with antibiotics and a host of other patent medicines, your body will never build up resistance and the next attack will just be worse.

There is one essential: protect yourself from the heat. Save your sun-tanning for the beach or the hotel swimming-pool. Otherwise, stay out of the sun. Wear a nicely ventilated hat and keep to the shade in the street. Try to do your open-air sightseeing in the morning and late afternoon. Take a siesta after lunch. Drink plenty of liquids – in the heat, dehydration is more of a risk than an upset stomach.

In all senses of the word, stay cool. In the first few days jet-lag, acclimatization and culture shock may lead you to lose your temper when you see the airports, railways and hotels not organized in a way you're used to, but don't forget, John Kenneth Galbraith called it a *functioning* anarchy. Therefore, count to ten and, like Delhi belly, it'll pass. Today you'll find airports, railway stations and hotels can be a pain anywhere.

Indians are mostly cheerful and will respond much more readily to a smile than a scowl.

The red tape can at times seem like barbed wire, but that, too, can be handled. Part of India's legacy of several centuries of bureaucracy (don't just blame the British civil service, it began long before) is an inordinate respect for the written document and the rubber stamp. Don't knock it – use it. Vouchers, passes, letters of introduction and printed businesscards all work like magic when a 'confirmed' reservation has become 'unconfirmed'.

If you should be travelling by train (see p. 239) and rate comfort above improvisation, go first class with an *Indrail Pass*. It saves you queues and gets you preferential treatment with reservations. Indian Airlines' *Discover India* is for 21 days of unlimited travel and is less economic than single tickets, but buy them *en bloc* with confirmed reservations that you should reconfirm at each new airport.

Echoing around every office you will hear the cheerful sentence: 'No problem' and if it rarely means what it says, you can interpret it as meaning 'no catastrophe' and have a good time anyway.

THE NORTH

The region around Delhi embraces the government capital; the heart of the old Mughal empire at Agra, and the nature reserves of Corbett and Bharatpur. In the Himalayan mountains there is the hill-station of Simla – which once served as the British summer capital – and the magic of Kashmir.

DELHI

On the Yamuna (Jumna) river at the western end of the great Ganga valley, the capital seems to have been a coveted place for India's conquerors. Though they each very often destroyed the work of their predecessors, the 20th-century city remains a fascinating compendium of India's imperial history.

Recent archaeological findings suggest that a site on the Yamuna river may have been the home of *Mahabharata* hero, Yudhishthira, dating back to 1000 BC. A rock-inscription from Emperor Ashoka indicates that Delhi was a major point on the trade route between the north-west frontier and Bengal in the 3rd century BC.

The Tomara Rajputs made it their capital in 736, with the name of Dhillika, and it was a focus of clan-wars until the Moslems conquered it and Qutb-ud-din Aybak set up his sultanate in 1206. Delhi was dismantled to make way for new monuments which then suffered from the devastating passage of Timur the Lame in 1398. He took away 90 elephant-loads of building materials and thousands of skilled Delhi stonemasons and sculptors to build his mosque at Samarkand. With the advent of the Mughals in 1526, Delhi alternated with Agra as the capital, and each ruler asserting his particular taste in architectural caprice.

Under the British, the town took a back seat to the ports of Calcutta, Bombay and Madras until 1911, when it became once more a proud imperial capital. No less vain than the Mughals, the new conquerors all added their own architectural caprices to New Delhi as a tribute to India's past but unmistakably British in overall conception.

Today, a tour of the capital takes you through a mixture of imposing ministries and embassies, modern office-blocks and hotels, and along the Old Delhi of vibrant Hindu and Moslem communities crowding in on the Mughal monuments. For more orientation, visit the Tourist Information Office on Janpath.

Delhi of the Sultans

Start at the southern end of the city, with the **Qutb Minarı**, a symbol of Islam's impact on India. Begun by Delhi's first sultan, Qutb-ud-din, and completed by his son-in-law Iltutmish, the 73-metre (240-ft) tower was erected to celebrate the Turkish conquest of Delhi.

The tower achieves its power with four storeys, each a tapering cylinder with angular and convex ribs, and separated by balconies.

In recent years, the top of the tower has been popular for suicide pacts by young lovers refusing to accept an arranged marriage. It is therefore off-limits; but the best bet for a panoramic view of the city is the top floor of one of the taller, more recent hotels.

The ruins of the ancient mosque **Quwwatu'l-Islam-Masjid** (which means 'The Might of Islam'), was built with the might of the Hindus. With no skilled Moslem labour at his disposal, Qutb called on the local craftsmen to build the mosque from the ruins of 27 Hindu and Jain temples, demolished by their own elephants.

You can see the results of this in the temple-pillars set on top of one another. Sculptures have been plastered over, but the Indian carving remains. Islamic architecture starts to come into its own with the five characteristic peaked arches of the prayer-hall screen, but even there the decoration, which includes the Arabic lettering, is naturalistic and Hindu in style.

In the mosque's courtyard, there is a 7-metre (22-ft) **Iron Pillar**, from the 4th century, brought here by the Rajput founders of Dhillika, but nobody knows from where. Unrusted after 1600 years worth of monsoon, this monument to the Hindu god Vishnu is said to have special properties: if you stand with your back against it and completely encircle it with your arms – no mean feat – good luck is yours for the rest of the day.

City of the Mughals

Due east of New Delhi's India Gate the much-plundered 16th-century **Purana Qila** (Old Fort) stands on an ancient mound, now believed to mark the site of Indraprastha of the *Mahabharata* epic.

The earliest Mughal building, the **Qal'a-i-Kuhna-Masjid**, with its minutely detailed moulding of graceful peaked arches, represents an important transition from the Turco-Afghan to the sophisticated stylistics of the Persian-influenced Mughals. The mosque was built in the year 1541 by Sher Shah, the Emperor Babur's General in office. **Sher-Mandal**, the octagonal tower due south of the mosque, serves as the General's pleasure-palace, but it was to be the death of his rival and successor, Humayun.

From this came the splendid monument located in Nizamuddin, the **Tomb of Humayun**, built by his widow Haji Begum and the inspiration for the Taj Mahal. Set back on a raised terrace in a set of walled-in tree-shaded lawns surrounded by hedges, but without the water once running in its channels ('rivers of life') and rectangular pools that were to be the perfect setting for the Taj.

Humayun's Tomb has a remarkable charm of its own, a repose and serenity in the delicate combination of materials used, such as buff and red sandstone and smart, grey-trimmed white marble.

With a majestic dome uniting the four octagonal kiosks over the terrace's latticed arches, this is the first fully-realised masterpiece of Mughal architecture. The numerous six-pointed stars, set in the abutments of the main arches, are not the Jewish Star of David but an esoteric emblem that you'll see all over the country.

> ### Stone Cold Stoned
> *Everybody thought that Emperor Humayun had kicked the opium habit when he got back from exile in Persia to reclaim his throne in 1555, but one day in the Sher-Mandal, which he had converted into a library for studying books on astrology and puffing a secret pipe, he was coming down the stairs, feeling more than a little woozy, when the muezzin at the local mosque started calling the faithful to prayer. Legend has it that the Great Mughal apparently tried to kneel right there on the staircase, tumbled over – and cracked his head. Fatally.*

DELHI

Dominating Old Delhi, the **Red Fort** was built by Shahjahan when he transferred the capital back to Delhi from Agra. Behind its ramparts, the Delhi citadel, is more a palace than a fortress with white marble preferred over the region's red sandstone. It's thought he used the same architect who worked on the Taj Mahal.

Coming from the south of the Fort, notice outside the Delhi Gate two monumental elephants. As part of the original design, they were destroyed by Emperor Aurangzeb, who refused images susceptible to idolatry. Viceroy Lord Curzon had the replicas reinstalled in 1903.

Enter the fort on its west side at the Lahore Gate. You find yourself in a vaulted bazaar street, an idea Shahjahan gained from Baghdad. Imagine administrators and Rajput princes riding on elephants through the arcade as far as the **Naqqar Khana** (Drum House), where the imperial band played and visitors were obliged to dismount.

Protesters at Delhi's Red Fort no longer risk a grand Mughal emperor sending out elephants to trample them.

68

Pass with the ghosts of those nobles and commoners through the drum house to the **Diwan-i-Am** (Hall of Public Audience). There, under a baldaquin with a statutory 40 pillars, the Emperor sat cross-legged on the throne, 'Seat of the Shadow of God'. He held audience at midday, surrounded by nobles while common petitioners attended in the courtyard below. As a visitor, you can admire the inlaid stone panels of birds and flowers at the back of the hall.

Entrance to the **Diwan-i-Khas** (Hall of Private Audience) was for the privileged by ticket only. You'll find it on the left, among the palace apartments on the Yamuna river. Beautiful as it is with its carved designs on the marble columns and cusped arches, imagine it in its full glory before the ravages of Nadir Shah in 1739, whose Persian troops chipped the gold out of its pillars and inlay off the ceiling and then carted away the fabulous Peacock Throne. Above the arches you'll see the inscription:

'If paradise on earth there be,
'Tis here, 'tis here, 'tis here!'

The last emperor to enjoy it was King George V, for whom a painted wooden ceiling was installed.

One of the few surviving palace apartments is the principal harem, **Rang Mahal** (Palace of Colour). The walls' paintings have gone and water no longer flows in its indoor Nahr-i-Bihisht (River of Paradise), but mosaics made of mirrors ornament the ceiling and walls of six boudoirs, a galaxy of stars when candle-lit (strike a match.) Southernmost of the palace buildings, **Mumtaz Mahal** was part of the imperial harem and is now a small museum of Mughal artwork.

To the north-west of the Diwan-i-Khas, the **Moti Masjid** (Pearl Mosque) is the one contribution to the Fort by Shahjahan's successor, Aurangzeb. Each evening, a sound and light show at the Red Fort tells its story; details from the Tourist Information Bureau.

Chandni Chowk, the road from the Fort's Lahore Gate, was once an avenue for processions. Today, it is the main thoroughfare linking Delhi's bazaars, selling jewellery, clothes and traditional sweetmeats.

On an outcrop of rock south-west of the Red Fort, Shahjahan's other great construction, the **Jama Masjid** (the great congregational 'Friday Mosque'), is the largest mosque in India.

The advisability of a morning or late afternoon visit on hot days will become apparent when you see the three pyramidal flights of stairs to the gate-houses. The 100-square metre (1,076-sq ft) courtyard is enclosed by long colonnades with a pavilion at each corner.

The prayer hall highlights the emperor's feminine aesthetic sense in the lotus calyx on the gateway's two lantern shafts, the delicately flaring balconies on the minarets, and the stripes to emphasize the bulbous marble domes.

Far in spirit from the Mughals but an integral part of Old Delhi, is **Raj Ghat**, the simple memorial to Mahatma Gandhi overlooking the Yamuna river. On lawns planted with the trees donated by visiting heads of state, the square of marble marks the place where Gandhi was cremated. A museum records the highlights of his life. The platform has an inscription recording his last words, *Hé Ram* (Oh, God), and nearby, a sign declares that most famous Gandhi talisman: 'Recall the face of the poorest and most helpless man whom you may have seen and ask yourself if the step you contemplate is going to be of any help to him.'

New Delhi

Nostalgics of the British Empire please note: Clive Road has been named Tyagraja, Queen Victoria Road has become Rajendra Prasad, and Curzon is Kasturba Gandhi.

Though the statues of British leaders have also disappeared, the British spirit remains in the city's planning. Faithful to the policy of separating the British cantonment from the Indian quarters with the

Victorian Vandals
Mongols and Persians weren't the only plunderers to hit Delhi. Most of the Red Fort's palace apartments were dismantled by the British to build army barracks after recapturing the city from the mutineers in 1857. This officially sanctioned vandalism has to be taken within the context of the vindictive climate reigning after the mutiny. Amends were made by the enlightened viceroys who were the first foreign rulers in India to protect and restore its patrimony. But Lord Curzon and company often had to contend with philistine circuit judges, who thought nothing of whitewashing or plastering over frescoes in a Mughal mausoleum while turning it into a rest-house.

71

barrier of a railway, the new city built for the Empire's Indian seat of government is separated from Old Delhi by the line running from Amritsar to Agra.

British Neo-classic architecture here is mixed with elements of Buddhist, Hindu and Mughal past and the geometry of its plan exudes the self-confidence of empire. As a visiting statesman once said of it: 'What splendid ruins it will make!'

The commercial pivot of New Delhi is the circular arcade and bustling roundabout of **Connaught Place**. With cinemas, banks, travel agencies, restaurants and the better craft emporiums, it's a place where the new name, Indra Chowk, does not seem to catch on.

Connaught Place straddles the north-east/south-west axis which links the Jama Masjid mosque of Old Delhi to India's parliament, **Sansad Bhavan.** Designed by the famous Herbert Baker, the rather too massive, colonnaded rotunda of the parliament building is at its best illuminated at night with an array of light-bulbs.

India Gate presents a proud but hazy memory of the British Raj.

The Viceroy's Residence, now the president's house, **Rashtrapati Bhavan** has wings radiating from the imposing grey-blue dome of the central block and the tranquil pools and lawns of its gardens, and so achieves the grandeur of Britain's heyday. From its artificial hill it looks down along the processional avenue, Rajpath (once Kingsway),

flanked by parklands, where India holds its march-pasts on Republic Day, January 26. At the other end of Rajpath stands **India Gate**, the war memorial to 90,000 Indian Army soldiers who died in World War I, designed by Lutyens in the style of a triumphal arch.

The strangest monuments, set in New Delhi south of Connaught Place, but historically in the 18th century of the Mughals' decline, is the **Jantar Mantar.** It is difficult to believe that these bizarre shapes, staircases going nowhere and windows in walls without rooms was built in 1724 by a serious student, rather than last century by some deranged architect hit on the head by his son's building-blocks.

It is in fact the astrologico – that is the astronomical observatory of Rajput prince Jai Singh II from Jaipur (see p. 100), where he built another and three more in Ujjain, Varanasi and Mathura. It's centre-piece is the right-angled triangle, Samrat Yantra (the Supreme Instrument), with a dome acting as a sun dial, 'accurate to half a second'.

Near here is what must surely be the liveliest Hindu temple of all, **Hanuman Mandir** (Temple of the Monkey God), a theatre, where you can witness the joyous atmosphere of popular Hinduism.

Tattoos for festive occasions are decorative but not indelible.

Hanuman is a beneficent deity predating classical Hinduism, and also the reason why no one would dream of harming the little lemurs (monkeys) running around here.

Museums

In what is artistically a predominantly Mughal city, the **National Museum**, on Janpath (Queensway) just south of Rajpath, is worth a visit for its collection of old Hindu sculpture, in particular those from medieval India of the kingdom of Vijayanagar.

Railway buffs will surely enjoy the display of the country's early steam engines at the open-air **Rail Transport Museum**. It is situated in the diplomatic neighbourhood of Chanakyapuri (behind the Bhutan Embassy). Adventurous as travel by rail in India still is today, one exhibit belongs hopefully in the past: the skull of an elephant that tried to derail a mail train in 1894.

Nehru Memorial Museum is devoted to the life of India's first Prime Minister and Independence. It is located in the house which Nehru inherited from the British Indian Army Commander-in-Chief on Teen Murti Road (it has sound and light shows in the evenings).

AGRA

With its Taj Mahal, Agra is the most popular sight to see in India. Even if the place had nothing else, it would be worth the trip, for the Taj, as one calls it affectionately, is a 'sight' that awakens the wonder and enthusiasm of the most blasé, worldweary traveller.

There's plenty more. Agra was the capital of Akbar the Great, the site of his fort, of his tomb outside the city at Sikandra and, a couple of miles west at Fatehpur Sikri, of the marvellous deserted town he built to celebrate the birth of a son and which he abandoned to fight on the north-west frontier. Heirs of the craftsmen originally brought here continue a tradition in jewellery, brassware, ivory and inlaid marble.

The first one hears of Agra is when Sultan Sikandar Lodi made it his capital in 1501. Babur captured it and the Koh-i-Nur diamond that is now in the British crown jewels. His grandson Akbar chose Agra for his capital over Delhi. In the 17th century, Jahangir made it a major focus of the Islamic world.

His son Shahjahan lost his taste for Agra after finishing the Taj Mahal for his wife Mumtaz-Mahal after she had died.

He moved the capital back to Delhi again in 1648, leaving the city's treasure to vandals, including the British after the 1857 Mutiny until the viceroys organized its restoration. Today it is the effects of pollution, which are taking their toll on Agra's monuments.

Getting There – and Back

Unless it's unavoidable, don't try to do Agra in one day. It's possible (and certainly better than missing it entirely), but it means you won't see much more than the Taj and, say, the Fort. More important, you might miss the unique beauty of the Taj as it changes in the light of different times of day.

If you are in a hurry, there's a flight from Delhi, but the comfort of an air-conditioned first-class seat on the Taj Express (3 hours) makes for an equally pleasant introduction to the big adventure of Indian railways. If you travel by car, avoid returning to Delhi after dark: the commercial traffic of goats and cows without any headlights is a notable risk for even a disciplined driver.

Alternatively, Agra is just one stop on the Indian Railways' most luxurious train, the aptly named 'Palace on Wheels' (for further info see p. 63).

Taj Mahal

This is truly a monument for all seasons. There are those who swear by *Sharad Purnima*, the first full moon after the monsoons, a cloudless midnight in October, when the light is at its clearest and also most romantic. Others love to see it in the middle of the heaviest monsoon, its marble translucent, and its image blurred in the rain-stippled water-channels of its gardens, but its magic is strong at any time of year, and any moment of the day. At dawn, its colour changes from milk to silver to rose-pink, and at sunset, it is golden. Observe it, too, in the brilliance of midday, for then it is utterly, dazzlingly *white*. On nights which have a full moon, the grounds stay open till midnight.

The **gateway** to the gardens of the mausoleum can be admired as a masterpiece in its own right, with its noble marble arches, the domed kiosks on the four corner turrets and two rows of 11 small *chhatri* (umbrella-domes) just above the entrance. It provides visitors with the perfect frame for a first view (and photo?) of the ensemble. You will find long-range photography is allowed, but it is forbidden to take pictures inside the monument.

The *chharbagh* (foursquare) **gardens** are an integral part of the Taj Mahal, both spiritually as the symbol of the paradis to which Mumtaz-Mahal has ascended and artistically to enhance the colour and texture of the mausoleum. The dark cypresses heighten the brilliance of the monument's marble, and the waterchannels, meeting at a broad central viewing-platform, not only provide a perfect second image, but also, with the reflection of the sky, add at dawn and sunset a subtle illumination from below.

Exquisite harmony and refined symmetry are the keynotes of the **mausoleum** itself. The structure is clad in miraculously white marble from the Rajasthan quarries of Makrana, achieving a magnificent texture with the subtly alternating broad and narrow slabs. Standing protectively at the four corners of the raised terrace, the minarets are deferentially slightly lower than the sublime central cupola.

Inside, the octagonal cenotaph-chamber contains the ceremonial marble coffins of Mumtaz-Mahal and also Shahjahan while, as was the custom of that time, the actual bodies are entombed in another chamber directly below.

You'll need to light a candle or use a pocket-torch in the cenotaph-chamber because daylight barely filters through the beautiful marble trellis-screens.

A Marble Requiem

Mahal means palace, but in this case Taj Mahal is in fact a short form of the name Mumtaz-Mahal ('Exalted of the Palace') which Shahjahan's cousin received when she married him. Daughter of his mother's brother, she had been his constant companion before he succeeded to the throne and then a 'first lady' among the hundreds in his harem. During 19 years of marriage, she bore him the grand total of 14 children, dying with the birth of the last, in 1631.

Shahjahan's beard – he was 39, one year older than his wife – turned white practically overnight and he continued to mourn for years, dressing in white on each anniversary of her death. The 12 years it took to build her mausoleum, working untiringly with his Persian architect and with craftsmen brought from Baghdad, Italy and France, may well be seen as the sublimation of his grief. 'Empire has no sweetness,' he wrote, 'for me now, life itself has lost all relish.'

Sadly, vandals removed all the tomb's spectacular treasures, but they left the gentle beauty of roses and poppies in rich inlaid stones of onyx, green chrysolite, carnelian and variegated agate.

The Taj Mahal – exquisite elegy in marble, eternally enchanting.

The mausoleum is flanked by two almost identical red buildings, to the west a mosque, to the east a guest-pavilion – each is a perfect viewing-point. Try the pavilion at sunrise and the mosque at sunset. But go round the back of the Taj, too, to the terrace which overlooks the Yamuna river. It has a view as far as the Agra Fort.

The Agra Fort

Built by Akbar in 1565, in a more embattled period than Shahjahan's Red Fort in Delhi, the Agra Fort was conceived as a citadel with a moat on three sides and its river on the fourth. Pleasure palaces were a secondary consideration and were in fact mostly additions by Akbar's successors.

The entrance from the south, at Amar Singh Gate, takes you up a ridged elephant's ramp, sloped to slow down any potential attackers. Pass into the long quadrangle of the piallried **Diwan-i-Am** (Hall of Public Audience). It was here that Captain William Hawkins handed Emperor Jahangir a special letter of introduction from King James I.

Due north is Shahjahan's **Moti Masjid** (Pearl Mosque). Climb the narrow staircase to the roof of the mosque for a fine view of the fort.

Just off the north-east corner of the Diwan-i-Am, the harem had its very own mosque, **Nagina Masjid**, and Hindu temple, and between the two a bazaar, where merchants sold silks and jewels. Near the *hammam* (baths), the **Diwan-i-Khas** (Hall of Private Audience) has rich carving and inlaid marble. The crack in the marble throne came from a British cannonball in 1857. As in Delhi's Fort, most of the private palace apartments face the Yamuna river. Among the most charming are the arcaded loggia and the gilt-roofed pavilions of the **Khas Mahal** or Private Palace.

A minute staircase led to the **Musamman Burj**, the pavilion of the emporer's chief wife. It is also popularly known as the 'Prisoner's Tower' for Aurangzeb imprisoned his father Shahjahan here, allowing him a view of his Taj Mahal.

The **Palace of Jahangir** is built around a square court with arches. There are Hindu motifs on the ceiling in the main hall, and in one on the west side: peacocks holding snakes in their beaks for example.

Other Sights

On the river bank opposite the fort is the **Tomb of Itimad-ud-Daulah**, overshadowed by the Taj Mahal. Built 15 years earlier by Jahangir's wife, Nur Jahan, for her father, who served as Mughal Prime Minister. There's a fragile elegance to the white marble pavilion's graceful silhouette, with its cupola and four octagonal turrets, topped by domed kiosks. The fine lattice-work on the arches and windows is superb, but its outstanding feature is the marble inlay, which is even more abundant than in the Taj and better preserved.

Akbar's mausoleum, located at **Sikandra**, is 10 km (6 miles) north of Agra. The best view is from the top of the gateway. On the cenotaph are the 99 names of Allah.

Fatehpur Sikri

In a country of crowded cities, it makes a refreshing change to travel 37 km (22 miles) south-west to an outcrop on which stands the citadel of Fatehpur Sikri, briefly Akbar's imperial capital.

Fatehpur, planned as a capital with Agra as a fallback position in case of attack, is protected on three sides by ramparts measuring about 6 km (4 miles). On the fourth side is an artificial lake stretching 8 km (5 miles) to the Rajasthan border, never sufficient, apparently, for the needs of the citadel and so one of the probable reasons why Akbar did not settle here permanently.

Built by the architects working on the Agra Fort, the citadel adds to the pink sandstone the darker red stone of the mountain ridge.

Entering via the **Agra Gate**, at the north-east corner, one passes on the right the *karkhanas* (work-shops) where carpenters, weavers and stonemasons worked.

In the **Diwan Khana-i-Am**, the courtyard used for public audi-ences, Akbar dispensed his justice attended by an executioner with instruments of torture and death. The sight of them was felt to be an effective means of getting at the truth. At the foot of the colonnade is a big stone tethering-ring for an elephant whose job it was to crush to death capital criminals.

Go through the pavilion to the **Daulat Khana** (Abode of Fortune) on the south side of the courtyard, a palace of which the most striking feature is the Hindu nature of its decoration: carved pedestals with stylized elephant heads as capitals, and sculpted stone screens.

In the south-east corner of the courtyard, the **Turkish Sultana's House**, or Hujra-i-Anup Talao (the Chamber of the Peerless Pool), the animals covering every wall panel and pillar create the illusion of woodwork rather than stone.

Fatehpur is subject to colourful stories in which it isn't possible to establish a historian's 'truth'. For instance, in the centre of the court-yard is the **Pachisi Court**, a huge chessboard for the game of *pachisi*, where Akbar and his friends are said to have used human 'pieces' – each player using a team of four slave-girls in different costumes.

To the **Astrologer's Pavilion**, in the north-west corner of the court, Akbar is said to have come for a daily dose of forecasts from the house-esoteric. The emperor is known to have consulted a whole panel of experts from Hindu and Moslem schools of astrology.

Just behind it is the **Treasury Pavilion**, where you can imagine him seated on cushions under the arches and counting the imperial money. The pavilion was known as Ankh Michauli (Blind Man's Buff), because it was where Akbar was thought to have played 'Hide and Seek' with his wives.

Akbar's capital is deserted, but merchants still do good business.

Hotly disputed is the purpose of the **Diwan-i-Khas**, not necessarily the hall of private audience that this implies. It is dominated by a great central pillar supporting a criss-cross of bridges to a balcony. Some claim it was here that Akbar held his famous debates with Jesuits, Brahmans, Parsi Zoroastrians, Sufi mystics, Jain and Buddhist monks, the sages arguing while Akbar sat listening, atop his pillar, or strode majestically around the bridges and balcony hurling his questions at his listeners. Others insist that it was just a storehouse for jewels. Truth in India, even more than beauty, is in the eye of the beholder.

Be careful on the steep climb to the top, but you'll find it is well worth it for the wonderful **view** across the citadel, particularly the palaces of the imperial harem to the south-west.

The harem's principal residence is **Jodh Bai's Palace**, built for Akbar's Hindu wife, the first royal spouse not required to convert to her husband's Islamic faith, and was Akbar's favourite residence at Fatehpur. It has one side screening out the summer heat while the other is open to the cooler breezes. Its most cherished feature is the turquoise ceramic tiling of the roof of the north and south wings.

Fatehpur's **Jama Masjid** (the Friday Mosque), at the south end of the citadel up on its mountain-ridge, was the very first of the open courtyard style mosques to became characteristic of all Mughal cities. Notice the carved central *mihrab* (the recess marking the direction of Mecca). The gleaming jewel of the red stone courtyard, however, is the marble-clad **Tomb of Shaikh Salim Chishti**. Its façade features black calligraphy, and in the ceno-taph-chamber there are pretty, painted flowers. Originally a more simple monument, its white marble

Walk across the courtyard to the beautiful five-tiered **Panch Mahal,** a palace with the Persian system of ventilation known as *badgir* (wind-tower): without walls on three sides, it is open for the breezes to sweep in. Each floor is supported on columns diminishing from 84 at ground-level to four on the roof. Notice that no two columns on the ground floor are alike.

'skin' was the addition of a very grateful Jahangir who, without the mystic Shaikh Salim Chishti, might never have seen the light of day.

Where Did You Go, Akbar?
The rise and fall of Fatehpur Sikri is the perfect illustration of Akbar's impulsive personality.

At the end of 1568, the emperor was 26 and still without a male heir. At the town of Sikri he met the Sufi mystic, Shaikh Salim Chishti, who promised him, given the proper spiritual dedication, not one, but three sons.

'In return for your friendship and grace,' said the emperor, 'I'll protect and preserve you. The Sufi replied: 'You can name your first son after me.'

The following August a boy was born, and was named Salim (later Jahangir). Akbar decided to move his capital to Sikri, and then waged a military campaign. Afterwards, he came back to add the name of Fatehpur (City of Victory) to the city.

By the year 1581 he abandoned Fatehpur, and only the family of Shaikh Salim Chishti remained, near the shrine Akbar had built. Today, some 16 generations later, they're still there, but there is no more sign of Akbar's people.

Bharatpur

Strictly speaking, Bharatpur is in Rajasthan, but its easy accessibility 42 km (26 miles) due west of Agra makes it logical to include it here. The marshes of the bird sanctuary of **Keoladeo-Ghana** offer a good change of pace. Even if you're not an avid bird-watcher, you'll enjoy the gentle walks in the woodland, with the chance of seeing exciting herds of nilghai antelope, black-buck and cheetal (spotted deer). A good time to visit is just at the end of the monsoon in October – when you can see flocks of storks, egrets and cormorants – and it is ideally combined with a full-moon trip to the Taj, but there's plenty to see all year round.

Among the over 300 different species of birds spotted here, you'll find eagles, cranes, pelicans, snake-birds, kingfishers, a host of ducks and geese, as well as a flock of rare wintering Siberian cranes between January and March.

The Maharaja of Bharatpur used to organize formal annual duck-shoots here for British viceroys and other top officials as well as for fellow princes. Today hunting is strictly banned. Bharatpur is only for the birds.

CORBETT PARK

Among India's nature reserves, this is the best known because of the audacious hunter of the man-eating tigers of Kumaon, Jim Corbett. The park was established in 1935 and was given Corbett's name after India became independent.

North-east of Delhi, this lovely park of forest and meadows by the Ramganga river in the foothills of the Himalayas is still the home of the tiger, leopard and elephant, as well as cheetah, sloth bear, wild pig, jackal and hyena. The river is stocked with plentiful mahseer and trout, as well as the occasional blind freshwater dolphin and two kinds of crocodile. Bird-watchers look out for stork, red jungle-fowl and black partridge.

The forest is thick with sissoo and tall sal trees, prized for their timber for ship-building. The great joy is an elephant-ride, swinging through the jungle and grassland reclining on a cushioned howdah. Rest at midday in the lodge at Dhikala and watch the elephants head down to the river.

Be sure to plan ahead through the Tourist Information Office or a Delhi travel agency because the admission to the park is by permit only. It is easy to obtain, however, and reserved accommodation can be booked either in the lodges or in the official camping-grounds.

Harems, the Cold Facts

The Indian Moslems' purdah *that separated women behind a screen in apartments, was derived from the old Persian institution of the harem. The armed security guards inside the harem were all female, no men, except for eunuchs at the outside doors.*

In Akbar's time, women were admitted to the harem as a great honour to their families, an imperial favour that was for some politically useful, but certainly not always nor even very often for the emperor's sexual pleasure. Though he might have several hundred 'wives', very few were his regular companions.

The senior wife, mistress of the household, was a person of great influence in the realm, guardian of one of the two imperial seals needed to authorize a new statute, the emperor's confidante in many of his decision. the most famous example was Mumtaz-Mahal, wife of Shahjahan, but much more powerful was in fact Jahangir's wife, Nur Jahan, who practically ran the whole country.

CHANDIGARH

The capital of the Punjab is just a stopover en route to Simla or a half-way stage en route to Kashmir. It's worth visiting this city planned in 1950 by Swiss-French architect Le Corbusier, who was invited by the Indian government to create a new city for the post-Partition Punjab on a windy plain at the foot of the Himalayas.

With British associate Maxwell Fry designing most of the housing, Corbu created the leading public buildings and laid out a town of spacious boulevards and sweeping tree-lined avenues, inspired at least

This cat has nine lives. You have only one, so keep your distance.

in part by Lutyens' ideas for New Delhi, and blessedly uncongested by growing traffic.

He planned the town on the principle of the human body, with the government buildings of the **Capitol** and university at its head, the commercial town-centre at its heart, and the industrial districts as its limbs.

In the **Assembly** building for parliament, the **Secretariat** administrative block, the vaulted **High Court** and the smaller **Governor's Residence**, you can see huge slabs of concrete like weathered granite from the nearby mountains. The buildings achieve ower by varying geometric with amorphous shapes, but also with bright colours visible behind the sub-breaker grilles.

You can enjoy a walk through the nearby **Rock Garden** of large, higgledy-piggledy concrete blocks and to the east, take a rowing-boat on the artificial **Sukhna Lake.**

At the time of going to press, the holy city of Amritsar and its Golden Temple are to remain off limits for the foreseeable future, but you can see Sikh architecture at another of their great national shrines, the Har Mandir Takht in Patna (see p. 161).

SIMLA

Similar to Chandigarh, this town, which is now capital of Himachal Pradesh, was built from scratch, back in the early years of the 19th century when the British colonial settlers were desperately searching for a refuge from the heat of the plains.

At an altitude of 2,130 metres (6,755 ft), it was once the place where a religious ascetic offered cool spring-water to the numerous weary and thirsty travellers coming out of the Himalayas. Some of them were British troops returning from the war with the Gurkhas of Nepal in 1819. They came back to build mountain retreats, as well as regular little cottages or perhaps an occasional grander mansion. From 1832 onwards, when Lord William Bentinck, governor-general, spent a happy summer here, it became the most prestigious hill-station. The viceroys made it their summer capital, including the famous Lord Mountbatten, who pondered the last details of Independence and Partition here in 1947.

The old reasons to head for the hills make a trip to Simla still more than valid, even if the old viceregal glamour has gone.

The air here is sweet, cool and clear and the pleasure of the quaint and tranquil English village atmosphere remains, along with some lovely walks into the surrounding mountains. You should, however, acclimatize to the altitude before attempting any long hikes.

In town, visitors can retrace the old favourite promenades along the shops of the **Mall** and see the old administrative offices of the **Ridge**. Where these two meet was what Kipling called 'Scandal Point'.

At the eastern end of the Mall you can see the **Gaiety Theatre**, old home of the Simla Amateur Dramatic Company famous for its productions of Victorian drama and Edwardian operetta.

The Ridge leads past the neo-Gothic Anglican **Christ Church**, where the bells are made from the brass of cannons captured from the Sikhs. At the end, you'll find the baronial pile of **Viceregal Lodge**, nowadays used by the Institute for Advanced Studies. In the grounds of the ivy-covered greystone mansion, you can imagine rickshaws pulling up for one of the viceroy's banquets. Peer into the grand hall with its elegant fireplace, coffered ceiling and majestic staircase. Can you imagine the musicians playing *Rule Britannia*?

Chandigarh's modern tapestries, a Punjabi pipe-dream?

Continue to the top of **Jakko Hill** where you can see a fine view of the town and valley.

High Jinks in the Hills

The British set up hill-stations wherever they could find a bit of reasonably accessible altitude – for Madras, Ootacamund (Ooty) in the Nilgiri Hills, and for the city of Bombay, Mahabaleshwar in the western Ghats. For Delhi and Calcutta, there was a choice of Simla, Mussoorie, Darjeeling, and many more. In the general relief at escaping the hell of the summer heat, they managed, in the classical British manner, to be very proper on the surface and naughty underneath.

In these last bastions of the British Raj, class thinking reared its head, with each hill-station having its own cachet, like the seaside resorts back home. Senior officers made the 'poodle-faking stations' off limits to subaltern – those, who were not permitted to watch their superiors poodle-faking with other men's wives. For, as Rudyard Kipling put it,

'Jack's own Jill goes up the hill
To Muree or Chakrata.
Jack remains and dies in the plains
And Jill remarries soon after.'

KASHMIR

The Vale of Kashmir, 1,700 metres (5,000 ft) above sea level, is one of those dream worlds, not just for the modern tourist, but of all time for the many conquerors who have passed through the deserts of Sind and the hot and dusty plains of the Ganga valley and heard tell of its blessed meadows, forests, full fruit orchards and lakes. It remains the undisputed treasure of the entire subcontinent.

Planning Your Kashmir Stay

Many people, particularly during high summer, make Kashmir the principal destination of their visit to India, combining it with perhaps just brief outings and daytrips in Delhi and Agra. However, if you're making a more extensive tour of India, it's a good idea to plan to see Kashmir at the end, when you can relax on a house-boat on a lake or go on a refreshing hike in the lush surrounding mountains.

In any case, for Kashmir more than anywhere else in India, it is truly imperative that you make all necessary arrangements for your travel and accommodation well in advance. During the peak holiday season, Srinagar flights are always

Not unusual to see the ladies doing heavy work with a smile.

heavily booked, so be sure to arrive in the country with reservations confirmed, including those for your return journey. Your travel agency can reserve you a houseboat, for a couple of days, allowing you to change around once you're fully settled in. One important and major advantage of advance reservations is that you'll be met at the airport straight away by a representative of the owner – it's not easy to find your own way among the boats.

Some visitors will prefer a hotel to a houseboat, but it would nevertheless be a great pity to miss out on this beautifully preserved relic

of the heyday of the British Raj in all its grandeur. In the 19th century, when Kashmir offered the most exotic hill-station of them all, the maharaja forbade the British to buy land there, so they then hit on the brilliant alternative idea of building luxuriously appointed houseboats moored on the lakes near Srinagar. Equipped and with all the Victorian upper middle class comforts the

colonials were used to, the more manoeuvrable smaller houseboats made their way to other lakes for duck-shoots or just for the pleasures of the cruise, while the larger ones stayed languidly put.

With so many new boats having been built in the same old style, with lovely Kashmiri carvings on the bridge and decks, many are too heavy to move around the waters,

The Himalayas are a heady site for skiing. Down in the valley they grow yellow colza for its oil.

but the traditional comforts are the same: woodburning stoves, plush armchairs in the living room, warm carpeting in the spacious bedrooms with superb personal service and fine Kashmiri cuisine, which you can enjoy on deck – note that you can arrange with the owner what you want to eat each day, Western or Indian style.

Most houseboats are moored on Dal Lake, but if you're seeking seclusion, there are others on the smaller Nagin Lake to the west. They are well serviced by *shikaras*, gaily decorated and roofed canoes somewhat reminiscent of Venetian

93

gondolas, plying their way around the lake, ferrying passengers. There is also a floating market of fruit and flowers, which has a flourishing trade in marijuana. The *shikaras* will also show you carpets, silks and shawls, as well as brassware, jewels, carvings, and tailors with names like Savile Roy, to recall their old British allegiance.

Srinagar

The heart of Kashmir's capital is built along the banks of the serpentine Jhelum river on the southern shore of the lakes.

Even if you have no intention of buying anything, the many bazaars, busy tailor's shops and government emporiums – one of them based in the handsome British Residency –

are fascinating places to observe the style, panache and neverending gall of that special Indian breed; that charming and often shameless scoundrel: the Kashmiri merchant.

A little shikara plies its way among the houseboats on Dal Lake.

Few monuments have survived Kashmir's troubled history, but the city's beauty lies in its numerous tranquil lakes and gardens. Take plenty of time for a leisurely cruise around **Dal Lake** and the adjoining **Nagin**, lounging on the cushions of a *shikara*. Enjoy the peace and quiet to ponder India's history, art and people.

As you coast along, under the weeping willows, travelling past the fishermen, you will pass among lovely **floating gardens** growing juicy fruits – melons, tomatoes and cucumbers – and lotus root in a mesh of reeds and mud floating in the water and moored in squares by four poles stuck in the lakebed.

On the western shore of Dal Lake, you will see the large white dome and minarets of **Hazratbal Mosque**, famous for its hair of the beard of the prophet Mohammed.

Look out for two small squares of land that rise up out of the lake: Sonalank, Akbar's Golden Island to the north, and Ruplank, Silver Island to the south.

Two hills, **Hari Parbat** to the north and **Shankaracharya** to the east of town, offer pleasant walks with the reward of a magnificent view over the lakes and the whole

95

Vale of Kashmir, 134 km long and 40 km wide (82 by 25 miles).

The **Mughal Gardens** are on the eastern shore of Dal Lake, and for Jahangir, if the Islamic idea of paradise had any meaning, it was here, amid the staggered terraces, tranquil pools, waterfalls and trees,

---

Beautiful Bone of Contention

Alexander left Greek settlements guarding the western frontiers of Kashmir and other Greeks filtered into the mountain-kingdom to account perhaps for the blue eyes and red hair of many kashmiris today. In the 3rd century B.C. Emperor Ashoka is said to have sent his Buddhist missionaries to found the town of Srinagar.

In medieval times, Kashmir remained, with a brief Mongol interlude, under Hindu kings until Afghans conquered it for Islam in the 14th century. WIth their equal enthusiasm for iconoclasm and creativity, they smashed the Hindu temples and introduced the arts of silk-weaving, shawl-embroidery, wood carving and ornamental papier mâché that have been the glory of Kashmir ever since.

Kashmir flourished under the Mughals, Akbar appreciating the sweet fruits of its orchards that he missed in the plains, Jahangir and Shahjahan laying out gardens that provoked the envy of Louis XIV when he heard about them. The Persian plunderer, Nadir Shah, couldn't resist laying claim to Kashmir but was soon replaced again by the Afghans. Supreme indignity for the Moslems came with the Sikh conquest led by Ranjit Singh in 1819.

The British did not help matters much nearly 30 years later when they took the state away from the Sikhs and handed it to a Hindu Rajput prince, under British protection, with Moselms forming an overwhelming majority of the population (today 68%). Moslem invaders tried to overthrow the Hindu ruler in 1947 and the latter, Maharaja Hari Singh, was rescued by the Indian Army only by agreeing to Kashmir joining India rather than Pakistan.

With hostility between India and Pakistan unresolved since a brief war over kashmir in 1965, no simple solution seems in sight. Today, with two-thirds of the original state in Indian hands and the other third, to the north and west, under Pakistani rule, many kashmiris have a "plague-on-both-your-houses" attitude, remaining, in spirit if not political fact, resolutely independent.

looking out over the lake against the backdrop of the Himalayas.

In summer, there's a sound and light show at Jahangir's favourite, the **Shalimar Bagh**, laid out a few

centuries ago, in the year 1616, and where you can relax as the emperor did, by lingering on the terraces to take in the changing perspectives of the scene before you.

The white marble pavilion on the first terrace was used for public audiences, and the second was a private pavilion, the third, made from black marble, for the harem,

Carpet merchants have found that the Srinagar bridges make good 'shop-windows'.

and the fourth was strictly reserved for the emperor's private use only.

Three kilometres (2 miles) to the south, **Nishat Bagh**, was laid out in the year 1633 by Asaf Khan, the brother of Jahangir's wife. With 12 terraces, it forms the largest of the gardens, lined with fine cedars and cypresses. It offers a magnificent view of the lake beyond.

Tucked away in a small fold of the hills is **Chashma Shahi,** the smallest but in many ways most exquisite of the gardens, drawing its water from a spring that runs directly down the mountainside.

Excursions from Srinagar

There are several easy day-trips to be made by bus or hire-car from Srinagar into the reaches of the surrounding mountains. If you're in the mood for a trek on foot, on pony or horseback – for which the local tourist information office can advise you on overnight camping facilities with guide and cook – there are two destinations which will provide visitors with decent accommodation as bases.

The resort **Pahalgam** is about 95 km (60 miles) east of Srinagar. The route there takes you through groves of willow, used for the local cricket-bat industry, and fields of saffron. If you wondered why it's so expensive, you need 150,000 of these purple or white crocus (only the stigma is orange) for a single (2 lb) of the stuff that flavours and colours those famous Indian curries and also Spanish *paella* – Spain is the only other place in the world apart from Kashmir where saffron is extensively grown.

The most popular journey from Pahalgam is 45 km (27 miles) up to the **Amarnath Cave**, which has an altitude of some 3,895 metres (12,742 ft). It is sacred to Hindus and so is a destination of devout pilgrimage on festive days for the sight of the imposing stalagmite called Shiva's lingam. Just 35 km (22 miles) from Pahalgam, but the most strenuous trek by far, is one leading to the spectacular **Kolahoi Glacier.**

Gulmarg, is 52 km (32 miles) west of Srinagar and is at about 2,653 m (8,622 ft) above sea level, It is currently developing its winter sports in addition to the golf and tennis which are already provided. There is wonderful hiking here, too, taking you through pine forests and meadows carpeted with wild flowers in summer.

THE WEST

The West is, above all, Rajasthan, land of the great maharajas, with its desert and lake palaces, but it's also the bustle of Bombay and the splendour of the cave temples at Ajanta and Ellora with the great bonus, further down the coast, of Mediterranean life Indian-style on the beaches of Goa.

Introducing Rajasthan

Rajasthan is undoubtedly one of the most romantic regions in India. Known as Rajputana, and stretching from Delhi to the Pakistani Sind and the Punjab, this land is where the Rajput warriors erected their desert and mountain redoubts. The palace-fortresses were built with granite from the surrounding hills, and with the dazzling marble used for the Taj Mahal.

The great cities of Jaisalmer and Jodhpur are on the ancient caravan routes from the Indus Valley to the Thar Desert, for this is a land of cattle-herders too.

One of their most spectacular monuments is the annual market-festival at Pushkar held each year in October (see p. 202).

Probably the descendants of the invading Scythians and Huns, the Rajputs formidable opposition met by the waves of invaders – Turks, Afghans or Mughals.

Despite the Rajputs' 'foreign' origin, their claimed 'descendancy' from the Aryan dynasties of the sun and moon was accepted by the Brahman priesthood and they were duly inducted retroactively into the *kshatriya* warrior-caste, a caste to which the Rajputs of today have continued proudly to adhere.

While the nearby Malwa and Gujarat came under Moslem rule, Rajputana remained Hindu. Towns with the suffix *-pur* had Hindu rulers; *-abad* is the Moslem suffix.

Some Rajput princes pursued an independent line. Others sent their daughters to the harem and to serve as officers in the imperial army. They enjoyed a privileged position during the time of the British Raj.

Elephants line up like taxis to take visitors around Amber fort.

JAIPUR

The capital of Rajasthan was built according to astrological precepts. Raja Jai Singh II, that scholar of the stars who dotted northern India with his collections of instruments for observing the heavens, chose an exact date for moving his capital from Amber – November 17, 1727 – as auspicious. He then layed it out according to the disposition of the stars and planets.

But let's begin at **Amber**, 9 km (5 miles) northeast of Jaipur, high up on a hill commanding a gorge, which offered military advantage but was not right for the expanded city he wanted for his capital.

> ### Land Survey at the Gallop
>
> *Jai Singh traced his ancestry back to the sun-dynasty of Ayodhya, with a grand sense of tradition. He asserted his independence of the Mughal empire by reviving the ancient Indo-Aryan practice of asvamedha, royal horse sacrifice. By this ritual, a king used to lay claim to all the land covered by a sacred white stallion let loose to roam for one year, followed by his warriors.*
>
> *Any neighbouring king who objected to his land being claimed in this way had to fight for the right to his own land.*
>
> *As a reward for its efforts, the stallion was mated, symbolically, with the king's wives and then cut up into quarters for a sacrificial meal.*

The road up to Amber takes you through classical Rajasthani landscape, its parched hills embracing Lake Maota, where water buffalo snooze lazily in the sun. You may also pass an occasional camel, that time-honoured method of transport known as the 'ship of the desert', incongruously hauling his load on a cart fitted with discarded tyres from an aeroplane.

At the **fortress**, the Rajputs of Jai Singh's Kachwaha clan slowed down their enemies with a steep elephant-ramp. You can travel by elephant up through the Suraj Pol (Sun Gate) to the **Jaleb Chauk**, a garden-courtyard swarming with langur monkeys and surrounded by elephant-stables.

A staircase zigzags its way to the **Temple of Kali**, wife of Shiva, and a Hindu goddess of death and of virginity.

The silver doors have *bas-relief* panels depicting her riding various animals. Her statue was brought from Bengal where the cult of Kali is particularly strong.

The **palace** is a subtle example of the maharajas' opulence: artists banished by Emperor Aurangzeb (see p. 34) worked on the columns and arches of the building, and on the gallery around the **Diwan-i-Am** (Hall of Public Audience).

The Diwan-i-Khas (the Private Audience Chamber), known as the **Shish Mahal** (Palace of Mirrors), features the Rajputs' flambouyant taste for covering all the walls with green, orange and purple glass and the vaulted ceilings with thousands of little convex mirrors. Strike a match to see the effect.

The most inviting place in the palace is the **Sukh Niwas** (Hall of pleasure), with its doors inlaid with ivory and sandalwood. Inside, cool water was brought down from the roof through a carved white marble chute, and fresh air was brought in through the finely chiselled lattice stonework.

The colour of its sandstone has gained for Jaipur the name of 'pink city' – although you will see that it changes colour with the season and time of day, from a rosy pink to warmest amber, to bright orange and dull ochre.

Appropriate for a descendant of the sun dynasty, Jai Singh laid out the city on an axis from the **Suraj Pol** (Sun Gate) in the east to the **Chand Pol** (Moon Gate) in the west, a main street that is today a lively bazaar.

The town's central focus was the most elaborate **Jantar Mantar** observatory, which was the final fruit of his labours and begun in Delhi (see p. 73). The initiated will appreciate the significance, others the mysterious atmosphere of its cream-coloured gnomons (the uprights of sundials), quadrants and sextants measuring

Chandra Mahal, directly south of the observatory, is the City's Palace with its mystically planned seven courtyards and storeys. A museum inside the building gives

Ladies watched from the Hawa Mahal windows but remained invisible.

an intriguing insight into the life and heyday of the maharajas: their rich costumes, their scimitars, and rifles inlaid with bright jewels and silver – and a horrible bludgeon with a double, serrated edge.

Jai Singh's observatories remain a puzzle to modern Indians.

Overlooking the street is the **Hawa Mahal**, literally the Wind Palace, but actually a rather grand, five-storeyed royal box, in which the ladies could sit and watch festive processions. Its airy, projecting oriel-shaped balconies are seen as a symbolic image of Jaipur style. There's a fine view from the top of the zigzag staircase.

JODHPUR

Of all Rajasthan's fortifications, Jodhpur's **Fort**, perched high on its sheer cliffs at the eastern edge of the Thar Desert, must surely rank among the most imposing.

The Rathor Rajputs built it in the 15th century and were always a belligerent bunch, bad trouble for Mughal foes and the Rajputs. Akbar decided it was better to have them on his side, rather than to try to convert them, typically, when he married the Maharaja of Jodhpur's sister, Jodh Bai, for whom he built a grand palace at Fatehpur Sikri (see p. 83-84), there was no question of converting her to Islam.

Near the east gate, you'll see tombstones where soldiers died in defending the fort, and cannonball scars indicating the Maharaja of Jaipur efforts to snatch a promised bride, Princess Krishna Kumari, not against her will. She took her own life during the battle.

On top of the *ramparts* the fort displays its proudest possessions a set of fierce-looking howitzers and a few cannons. From here there is a fine view of the blue and white-washed city.

Behind the ramparts and gates, with their sharp iron spikes to stop elephants ramming them, is a very handsome residential palace.

It's majesty is most notable in the balconies of the **Royal Harem**, which have balcony screens of the most delicate latticework.

The palace **museum** displays a colourful collection of exhibits, giving an insight to the daily life of those who lived there: there are luxuriously embroidered elephant howdahs, as well as babies cradles and ladies' palanquins (an oriental version of a sedan-chair). Some of these were completely closed up

---

What, No Jodhpurs?

Those celebrated riding breeches, now worn by riding fans all over the world, were quite the fashion for hunters in northern India, but it was in fact the Maharaja of Jodhpur who brought them over to London for Queen Victoria's Diamond Jubilee. Or rather, he didn't bring them, they got lost in a shipwreck and he had to get a London tailor to make a new pair. The secret of their peculiar design was out and they became all the rage among English horsemen, along with the dapper maharaja's ankle-length riding-boots, known as jodhpurs, and his close-fitting Jodhpuri coat.

so that the bride was completely invisible, while others were made for when she was truly married, and so were made with a peep hole to allow her to be seen

At the **Iron Gate** exit, you'll see on the wall a more poignant side of life as a maharaja's wife – 15 scarlet coloured *sati* handprints of the widows who threw themselves

onto their husbands' funeral pyres in ritual sacrifice, in keeping with the tradition of the era.

In the bustling old city centre of Jodhpur city itself, you can't and shouldn't miss the bustling life of **Saddar Market** situated by the old clock-tower.

Under the banyan tree any one of a dozen barbers will be happy to give you a shave and a haircut – and a good deal of local gossip into the bargain. In the market proper, the spices and grain are piled up in multi-coloured mountains, and the merchants chant as they measure out separate lots of five kilos each: 'three, three, three,' and 'four, four, four' and 'five, five, five'. At every corner you turn, the fort looms on the horizon, a constant reminder of the town's war-torn history.

Just 8 km (5 miles) due north of Jodhpur, in a pretty park on the site of the old capital of *Mandor*, is the maharajas' mausoleum.

Watched over by crows, pigeons and parakeets – and some rare birds, which will doubtlessly be of interest to ornitholopgists – are a number of temple-like memorials built on the site of the maharajas' funeral pyres, and a colonnade of Hindu god-heroes.

The Rajputs outdid the Mughals in their taste for riotous colour.

If you're going to Jaisalmer by road, it's worth a detour to **Osian** to see the Hindu and Jain temples, many of them dating as far back as the 8th century. Somehow this sculpted pantheon of Hindu deities and Jain prophets has survived the sometimes ferocious elements of India's weather and Mahmud of Ghazni's iconoclasts.

Back on the road to Jaisalmer, there is one last splash of colour to delight the senses before you plunge into the desert: the fields are dotted with mounds of bright colour – red hot chilli peppers – before you plunge into the stunning contrast of the desert.

JAISALMER

Situated on the route of the ancient caravans that brought goods from the Middle East and Central Asia, the sandstone citadel of Jaisalmer, protected by an imposing double set of bastions, rises like a mirage from the sands of the Thar Desert.

Jaisalmer was founded by the Maharawals, in the year 1156, and is the oldest of the fortified cities of Rajasthan. Though much of the city has grown up outside the **fort** – modern in time, but not in style – 3,000 people live within its walls.

Some of their houses in the side streets are from the 12th century. The best view of the whole citadel can be had from the terrace of the Jaisal Castle Hotel.

The elaborate sculpture which can be found in four 15th-century **Jain temples** within the fort finds its counterpart in the finely carved façades of the **Merchants' Havelis** (mansions), built 200 years later, and sheltered from sandstorms on the north-east side.

Much more than the individual monuments – handsome but none of them grandiose in the restricted spaces available – it is the general atmosphere of the town: that gives it its special magic, everything here is bathed in a serene desert light

Women of the desert that around Jaisalmer's fort recall the Arabia of biblical times.

that adds a shimmer to the stone and a translucence to the shadows. To see the **desert** at its best, go out at dawn and at sunset.

Titles and Titles

Rajput princes attached major importance to titles. They were first named Rao, *'chief' of their clan. Akbar called them* Raja, *'King'. Thereafter, they promoted themselves to the grand title of* Maharaja, *'Great King' or the* Maharana, *and* Maharaja Dhiraj, *'Great King of Kings', or even* Maharaja Dhiraj Raj Rajesur, *which is something like 'Great Hero King of all Kings'. You might think it would stop there, but then came the British with their 'Knight of the Garter', and 'Knight Commander of the British Empire'– and more.*

The princes began to count their titles, the important issue being the number of initials. A major State crisis could arise if one received a CVO (Companion of the Victorian Order) when a rival received a KCVO (Knight Companion etc.). The Maharaja of Jaipur, for instance, died happy in the year 1970 as Lieutenant-General HH Maharaja Sir Man Singh Bahadur, GCSI, GCIE.

Beyond Jaisalmer you'll find the road peters out at the village of Sam and the forbidden area of the Indian military installations on the border with Pakistan. On the way to the village you'll come across a 'camel-station', from where you can take a camel ride.

For fans of this quaint form of transport, longer camel-safaris can be set up through Jaisalmer travel agencies.

Ask the camel-driver to direct you to the still uncharted village of **Kuldhara** – uncharted because it was one of 84 villages abandoned over 160 years ago by the clan of Paliwal Brahmans who, after living there for centuries, left suddenly during the night, rather than having to face paying the new, arbitrary land-tax. It still stands as a ghost town – groups of dilapitated square hosues made from sandstone – and is visited nowadays only by the occasional goatherd, who will play you a tune on his flute in traditional style.

Just 9 km (5 miles) out of town, **Mool Sagar** gardens are a popular place for picnics in the rainy season. There are pretty arbours and a monsoon-pavilion, but it is in fact pleasant all year round.

UDAIPUR

If Jaisalmer is the city of the desert, then Udaipuris is its opposite: the city of lakes and gardens.

The lakes are either reservoirs or tanks created by the Maharana Udai Singh for his new capital by damming up the Berach river after Akbar had ransacked his mountain redoubt at Chittorgarh.

The Maharanas of Udaipur, had five palaces in and around Udaipur: the City Palace for winter quarters, the Jagniwas in Lake Pichola used as a summer palace (now the Lake Palace Hotel), then the Jag Mandir

Jaisalmer sandstone balconies are prodigies of intricate carving.

on Pichola, used for celebrating festivals, the Lakshmi Vilas Palace for guests beside the lake, Fateh Sagar, and a monsoon palace up in the Aravalli Hills. It was the marble used for them that Shahjahan chose for his his Taj Mahal.

Lake Pichola, 4 km (2 miles) long and 3 km (2 miles) wide is the largest. Cruises are available from the Bhansi Ghat, which is near the City Palace. This will enable you to travel out to the **Lake Palace Hotel**, even if you're not staying there. The southern end of Pichola has the best **view** of the lake, taking in the two island-palaces and the City Palace beyond.

The 16th-century **City Palace** on the east shore of the lake is now a museum. The sun symbol of the maharana is everywhere, a source of worship during monsoons. The armour displayed includes an outfit for disguising horses as elephants. The frescoes illustrate the tragic story of Princess Krishna's suicide at Jodhpur. The glass baubles in the mosaics – which are as big as golf balls – have replaced real jewels.

North of the City Palace is the handsome **Jagdish Temple**, a rare example of Indo-Aryan style and symbolic of it's independent spirit.

The town's **Folk Museum** has an excellent display of Rajasthani art, which includes bright puppets, costumes and the whole range of different-coloured turbans worn by the various Rajput clans.

Fateh Sagar Lake is reached by boat at the north end of Pichola, but it also makes a pleasant drive past the gardens of bougainvillea and lilac of Lakshmi Vilas Palace.

You can also visit the **Gardens of Saheliyon-ki-Bari** (Maids of Honour), where the maharana kept the Moslem dancers presented to him by the Mughal emperor.

The gardens here are famous for their five fountains which imitate the many different sounds of the monsoon, from light showers to torrential storms, and which are an integral part of Indian life.

Perennial water-carrier takes a shower in Udaipur's Lake Pichola.

Chittorgarh is a fortress and the site of the Rajputs' many acts of sacrifice. Making a good trip by road or rail from Udaipur, it is on a plateau some 150 m (487 ft) in height up in the Aravalli Hills.

Entering the north-western side, you can go through seven gateways to see the remains of the Rajput's heroic exploits. Stones mark where they fell in battle.

The key to Rajasthan's mystery is the desert, and its faithful guardian is the camel.

South of the Main Gate is the 15th-century **Palace of Kumbha**, built over the cave where Padmini led the first *jauhar* and to which the Rajputs' descendants return for an annual celebration. Some of the walls in the palace were built with pieces of stone that were removed from Buddhist temples and brought here from a village.

Kumbha's **Jaya Stambha** (the Tower of Victory) is 37 m (120 ft) high and was built to celebrate his great victory over Sultan Mahmud Khalji of Malwa in 1440.

The tower's nine storeys are decorated with Hindu dieties, but otherwise it seems inspired by the **Kirti Stambha**, a Jain Tower of Fame, built in the 12th century.

At the southern end, beside a pond with a pavilion in the middle, is **Padmini's Palace**, where the princess is said to have passed her last days. It is unlikely that the mirror in the room overlooking the pond was the very one in which the sultan got his fatal peek at her, but it helps the guides to tell the story and entices visitors to ponder it.

Do or Die

Rajput warriors placed a high price on their honour. In 1303, Sultan Ala-ud-din of Delhi laid siege to Chittorgarh, it is said, to win for his wife the Princess Padmini, whose beauty he'd been allowed to glimpse only in a small mirror, but rather than submit to this, the Rajputs' wives and daughters committed jauhar, that is mass self-immolation, while warriors rode out of the fort in the saffron robes traditionally worn for the last battle unto death.

Over 200 years later there was another heroic resistance against the Sultan of Gujarat, ending in another tragic jauhar, in which 13,000 women are said to have died – and 32,000 saffron-clad Rajputs. The last stand came with the devastating attack by Akbar in 1567, and one last suicidal sacrifice and battle.

115

RANAKPUR

Hills and mountains are especially sanctified in the cult of Jainism. In fact, you will find in the Aravalli Hills, situated in the south-western part of Rajasthan, one of the Jains' leading sanctuaries.

North of Udaipur, a mountain road takes you past green terraced fields and mango groves over the deepest ravines to the magnificent white marble temple-complex of Ranakpur.

Chaumukha Temple is known nowadays as the quadruple temple because of its four central domes, within a big complex of 84 domed shrines, each one topped by a flag tinkling its bells in the wind – a gentle musical homage to the many deities worshipped inside.

Built in 1438, the Chaumukha is dedicated to Adinath, Jainism's original 24 Tirthankaras (teachers) whose truths were revealed by **the prophet** Mahavira (see p. 56–57).

As with all the holy places of Jainism, you must remove not only your shoes but any goods of leather that you may be wearing.

Walking through the entrance hall, decorated with a number of sensual sculptures, and across the half-moon threshold, you penetrate a positive forest of pillars, all of them symmetrically aligned, but each subtly different in its intricate carving.

The 15th-century temple's rich carvings attest to the wealth of the Jain merchant who commissioned it. You can find him sculpted, set on the 2nd row of pillars, 2nd pillar from the left in a position of prayer facing the statue of Adinath. His architect, Deepa, is also there, in the 3rd row of pillars, 1st pillar on the right. Restoration work on the temple is, amazingly, carried out by the 14th generation of Deepa's direct descendants, alive today.

You can climb up to the roof for a fascinating perspective of the flags, domes, and trees surrounded by the Aravalli Hills.

The Dilwara Temples are sited on **Mount Abu**, in a former hill-station for the British (now used by the Indian bourgeoisie). If you go – and the temples are well worth it – you would do best to take the train from Jaipur or Ahmedabad.

After the arid desert of the plains, the lush green cornfields of the Aravalli Hills are a welcome sight.

AJANTA AND ELLORA

The cave temples hewn from the granite of the Vindhya mountains in the north-west of Deccan are one of the great wonders of India.

They are masterpieces since the 'caves' are man-made hollows in solid rock, from which a complex of architecturally elaborate temples and monasteries has been carved with simple instruments.

Even beyond this *tour de force,* the rock-cut sanctuaries of Ajanta and Ellora are superb works of art – sensuous painting and expressive sculpture of the highest order.

Both are within easy reach of the town of Aurangabad. Try not to visit both sites on the same day. If you are interested in following the historical evolution of the temples, stop off at Ajanta first, where some caves are from the 2nd century BC. Reserve Ellora for a tour during the afternnoon, when its caves will be illuminated by sunlight. Reliable official guides from the office of the Archaeological Survey of India offer their services free of charge.

Ajanta has the advantage over Ellora, remaining untouched for 1,000 years until British soldiers discovered it during a tiger-hunt in 1819, while Ellora's caves were in constant use as dwelling places.

The use of rock-cut sanctuaries goes back to the time of Emperor Ashoka, during the 3rd century BC, when itinerant Buddhist monks formed a religious order and the emperor provided them with rock-hewn cells as a retreat, *vihara,* in the monsoons. The monks added a hall for worship, *chaitya* or temple.

Of the 29 caves, all of them Buddhist, five are *chaitya* temples and the rest, *vihara* monasteries. Cut from a horseshoe-shaped cliff standing 75 m (252 ft) high above a narrow gorge with small stream running through it. Originally, each *vihara* had its own stairway down to the stream.

The caves have been numbered from 1 to 29, west to east. Just nine of them will give an impression of the whole. Start in the middle, at the oldest, then work your way east before returning to the historically later caves at the western entrance.

Cave 10 is probably the oldest of the *chaitya* temples, dated at about 150 BC. Its nave and aisles are divided by 39 octagonal pillars leading to a *stupa,* the domed focus of veneration, with an apse beyond, permitting the circumambulation. There is no representation of the Buddha in this early era.

Cave 9, is a sanctuary from the 1st century BC and is smaller than No. 10. It is dominated by the *stupa*. The two-storey façade with arched window and Buddha figures in side niches was probably added in the 6th century AD.

The monastery of **Cave 12**, will give you an idea of the monks' sleeping-quarters. Those who are not afraid of the dark, can go in and lie down on one of the stone beds in the *vihara's* 12 little cells.

Two elephants welcome you in a kneeling position to **Cave 16**, one of the most important of the later caves created between AD 475 and AD 600. The Mahayana school of Buddhism encouraged worship of a Buddha image, which is why the *stupa* was replaced with a sculpture of Buddha sitting in a posture used traditionally for teaching. Look out for the two sculptures of amorous couples on the ceiling.

With the richness and vigour of its mural mural paintings, **Cave 17** represents the summit of Ajanta's artistry. From the 5th century AD, the walls show the 12 stories of Buddha's enlightenment.

Buddha's steadfast resistance to temptation gave the painters of that time a splendid pretext to show the sensual side of court-life as a foil to the Master's spirituality. We see him taming an enraged elephant or, appearing as the warrior Simhala attacking the Island of Ogresses, while his wife Rani, who is holding a mirror, languorously prepares her toilet, with hand-maidens holding her cosmetics.

The sculpted Buddha is seen with the wheel symbolic of his law and two deer referring to the park at Sarnath where he held his first sermon. On the pedestal, look out for two other, smaller figures, one of which is holding a bowl for alms or offerings – they represent the rich merchants who financed the cave's construction.

The small *chaitya* of **Cave 19** is notable for the carved façade and Buddha statues of its interior, and the graceful figures relaxing in the side niches at the entrance. Visit **Cave 26** for a riot of 'architectural' bravura – the elaborately ribbed vaulting, finely carved pillars and a truly Baroque shrine with seated Buddha.

Unlike the early, rather austere monasteries, **Caves 1 and 2** are

119

richly ornamented, and again there are superb murals of bright-eyed deer, as well as peacocks, monkeys and elephants and the opulent life, with Prince Siddhartha riding away on horseback. The masterpieces, though, are in Cave 1: two spiritual Boddhisattvas on the back wall on either side of the ante-chamber.

The caves of **Ellora**, are cut out of a whole hillside of basalt rock, and conceived on a much grander scale than Ajanta's. Local villagers have constantly sheltered in them during monsoons or epidemics, so that the murals have disappeared, but the magnificent sculpture has survived.

Starting where Ajanta left off – some of the Buddhist artists may well have moved over to Ellora – all of the 34 caves were created between the 7th and 12th centuries. The first 12 of them are Buddhist, 17 of them are Hindu, and the other five are Jain.

They stretch north-south over 3 km (2 miles), allowing you the option of climbing behind some of them as well as approaching from the cave-entrance.

The most important Buddhist excavation (1–12) and only *chaitya* sanctuary here, is the 8th-century Cave 10 with a fine, rib-vaulted ceiling reminiscent of a western Romanesque cathedral. The great Buddha seated in the domed stupa is worshipped by Hindu artisans as Visvakarma, carpenter of the gods, so that the sanctuary is known as the Cave of the Carpenters.

Cave 12 consists of a *vihara* dormitory with three storeys. Its sensual, feminine sculptures show growing Tantric Hindu influence. You must imagine these originally painted in bright colours.

> **Cut and Paste**
> *Unfinished caves such as 14 or 24, show that the sanctuaries were 'created downwards', that is hewn out of the cliff rather than being built up from floor to roof. Among the many other differences which distinguish these caves from more conventional architecture are the columns and arches – it might perhaps be more appropriate to speak of sculptured roof-beams – which did not fulfill a weight-bearing function here.*
>
> *The wall paintings are often wrongly described as frescoes, in which paint is applied to a damp plastered surface, whereas here, the technique is that of tempera, paint on a dried surface of plastered cow-dung.*

Of the Hindu temples (13–29), **Cave 14** is an interesting transition from the Buddhist caves because in the pantheon of Hindu gods, Vishnu sits in a meditative pose suggesting he was converted from a Buddha. Another two are similar to the Bodhisattvas of Ajanta. The sculpture shows a dynamic Shiva killing demons and playing dice in the Himalayas; a group of boys

Ajanta cave-painting depicts the sensual life that Buddha left behind him.

playing with the sacred bull; and mother goddesses with children.

The masterpiece of Ellora, is the **Kailasa Temple** of Cave 16. With a ground plan the size of the Greek Parthenon and a structure half as

121

tall again, this was the work of the 8th-century Deccan king Krishna I.

In the process of shaping the temple and its shrines in an area 82 m (265 ft) long and some 47 m (150 ft) wide, and leaving the back 'wall' of the courtyard 30 metres (97 ft) high, an amazing 200,000 tons of rock were cut away from the face of the hill.

Whatever was saved in hauling the masonry needed to 'erect' such an edifice was more than counter-balanced by the seven generations of craftsmen who completed their amazing carvings *from one piece of rock*. The anonymous sculptors created a panoply of Hindu tradi-tion – legendary heroes and their battles, hunts and weddings.

The result is a Hindu temple on a grand scale which can be easily compared with its inspiration: the many temples of Mahabalipuram (see p. 189), built some 50 years before in the southern region.

The huge gateway leads to the *mandapa* worship hall, with the tall pyramid of the shrine beyond, the whole structure symbolizing in stone the mythical Mount Meru, Himalayan home of the gods.

After seeing the sculpted friezes at courtyard level, you can gain yet another perspective of the temple's fine detail from above, by walking along the stone ledge that leads around the top. Be assured that there's no risk with good shoes and the safety railing.

After Kailasa, the Jain caves (nos. 30–34), excavated between the 8th and 13th centuries, will come as an anti-climax – and this despite the considerable prowess of their sculptors.

Cave 31 tries to emulate the style of the great Hindu temple on a much smaller scale, but the artists here were working on much harder rock and so abandoned their effort. The most interesting of all remains the two-storey **Cave 32**, known as Indra Sabha, and notable for the upper floor's extravagant carving the hallmark of Jain sculptors, and the great elephant, more rigid than Kailasa's – because of the tougher stone, but somehow more noble.

A temple built not from the ground up, but hewn from a granite cliff.

BOMBAY

Bombay's Gateway of India still describes the town's main function. For those who want to work their way down to the south, Bombay is still, as it was for the servants and soldiers of the British Empire, the natural gateway.

An occasional luxury liner does still glide past the great stone gateway, the harbour promenade of the Apollo Bunder and the Yacht Club to dock at Ballard Pier. For the rest of us landing at Santa Cruz Airport, the old turmoil of dockside porters and rickshaws that once submerged the newcomer has been replaced by the equally crazy bustle of businessmen and workers going to and from the Gulf.

With skyscrapers shooting up, Bombay is the busiest industrial and commercial centre in India – cars, textiles, chemicals, nuclear energy and shipping – and a focus for the cinema and the renewal of Indian art, but this huge wealth is juxtaposed with abject poverty epitomized by women with bricks on their heads for building luxury apartments, and sack-cloth hovels on construction sites.

For anyone who is not here on business, three days, at most four, should be enough to get a good idea of this exhausting city – with the possible exception of nostalgics of the British Raj, who will find a wealth of intriguing relics.

Before exploring the sprawling city stretching in a wide crescent over 20 km (12 miles) from north to south, go to the Government of India Tourist Information Office which is situated opposite Churchgate Station.

Then begin just where King George V himself did on his visit back in 1911, on the promontory at the end of Apollo Bunder, a site marked today by the world famous **Gateway of India** – a monument moving for its symbolism rather than beauty, depending on how you feel about the British Empire it was built to celebrate.

Kipling insisted in his *Ballad of East and West* that 'never the twain shall meet', but the British have done their best by perching four Gujarati domes on this otherwise very Roman concept of a triumphal arch. This edifice was inaugurated in the year 1924, with the Somerset Light Infantry marching through it with solemnity to their ships some 24 years later. They were the last British troops to leave India.

Kipling's Cradle

Rather than Delhi, Bombay is the place for Raj-buffs to start out, for this was the beginning of the British imperial adventure in India. Once a chain of swampy, malaria-ridden islands inhabited by a few fishermen and peasants tapping toddy from the palm trees, it didn't seem a great loss to the Sultan of Gujarat when he ceded it to the Portuguese in 1534. They passed it on to the British as part of Catherine of Braganza's dowry to Charles II in 1661. The East India Company picked it up for a song – a rent of £10 a year for the next 62 years.

After years of intimidation by the Portuguese, the Hindu, Parsi and Jewish merchants flocked into the burgeoning port city. The swamps were dried out and linked by land-fill to form one Bombay Island, separated from the mainland by the easily bridged Thana Creek. Modern docks were built, the first cotton mills in the year 1853, followed quickly by other factories to instal Bombay's own industrial revolution. The bard of the Raj, Rudyard Kipling, son of the local art school teacher, was born here in 1865. Bombay was British India's naval kingpin and, as you will see from the many warships sitting in the harbour, remains today the headquarters of the Indian Navy.

Facing the gateway is the Indian equestrian **statue of Sivaji**, erected in 1961 to honour the Maratha hero of Hindu nationalism who fought against the Mughals (see p. 34).

Beside him is the **Taj Mahal Hotel**, also monument, built by a member of the Parsi industrialist dynasty, the Tatas. Architecturally it's another mixture of Western and oriental styles, and a surviving part of the old traditional tour that took world travellers from the West to Shepheard's in Cairo, Raffles in Singapore, the Peninsula in Hong Kong and the Imperial in Tokyo. You can get a whiff of the old romance by taking tea in the Sea Lounge for the harbour view – and recall the dizzy *ingénue* in the bar who thought that the mausoleum at Agra was named after the hotel.

'The Raj District'

Going north-west from the Taj, in the area around the Maidan that was the heart of British Bombay, connoisseurs appreciate the architecture that fans call 'eclectic' and foes 'mongrel'.

The old Secretariat is mostly described as Venetian Gothic, the University Library French Gothic, the Telegraph Office Romanesque, the High Court and the Cathedral of St. Thomas as Early English. The architects were British but the artisans were Indian, and adept at adding detail reminiscent of Rajput forts and Mughal palaces.

On the octagonal spire of the University's **Rajabai Clocktower**, the national overtone is stressed with 24 figures representing the castes of the Maharashtra State, of which Bombay is the capital.

In the **Cathedral**, even the most anti-imperialist may be touched by some of the poignant epitaphs for those who died in the military or civil service of their country.

For big Raj-buffs, the supreme example of Indo-Gothic style is the *Victoria Terminus*, affectionately abbreviated to VT nowadays, once *the* railway station that launched adventures inland, now handling suburban traffic.

North-west of the VT is the bustling **Crawford Market** (post-Independence known as Mahatma Jyotiba Phule). Behind the brick façade with *bas-relief* friezes by Kipling's father over the gate, the stalls still have the original layout with vegetables to the left; fruit and flowers to the right; fish, mutton and poultry and straight ahead.

The Indians' Bombay

Beyond Crawford Market, the area that the Indians truly call their own, away from the Apollo Bunder and the Maidan, still redolent of their old imperial masters, is known in tribute to simple reality as the City.

This is the heart of Bombay's teeming street-life, where Indians from the entire subcontinent compete with lively Maharashtrans in **bazaars.** Among the extravagantly coloured Hindu temples and subtle mosques of the Moslem neighbourhoods, Jain merchants sell gold in the Zaveri Bazaar, while others sell silver, brass and copper, leather and lace. The most notorious of these is the Chor (Thieves') Bazaar, where car-owners can buy back their own spare parts, as well as the 'Gucci' luggage, and where the 'Cartier' watches have in fact never been west of Bombay.

The Indians' Bombay is also epitomized by the promenade of **Marine Drive**, around Back Bay from Nariman Point to the residential area of Malabar Hill. It's unlikely, though, that you'll see the

Bombay's Dhobi Ghat, the world's biggest open-air laundry.

Towers of Silence, where the Parsis expose their dead to the vultures.

What you should see, however, is **Chowpatty Beach**, which is not for swimming or sunbathing. It's one of the greatest people-watching spots of western India: fakirs and fakers walking on fire, sleeping on nails, climbing ropes in midair or burying their heads in the sand, food-vendors hawking *kulfi* ice cream, as wel as *pan* betel-chew and *bhelpuri*, a speciality of spicy vegetables.

Museums

The **Prince of Wales Museum**, at the southern end of Mahatma Gandhi Road, has a collection of miniatures and 7th-century sculptures from the caves of Elephanta, as well as a pottery and stone tools.

The new **Jehangir Art Gallery**, immediately behind the Museum, shows the trends in modern Indian painting, two of the most important artists from Bombay being Tyeb Mehta and Akbar Padamsee.

In Victoria Gardens, one animal to see is the stone elephant from Elephanta Island. It belongs to the **Victoria and Albert Museum** nearby, showing the old history of Imperial Bombay.

More up-to-date, the Tourist Information Office can organize a visit to the set of a Bombay **film studio** to watch one of their huge, romantic productions in progress.

Elephanta

The 7th-century cave-temples of Elephanta Island make a pleasant boat-excursion by ferry from the Apollo Bunder. Look out for the nuclear reactors at Trombay.

Known as Gharapuri, Sacred City of the Kings, the island was named Elephanta by Portuguese sailors, and although their musket-practice damaged many sculptures of Hindu gods in the caves. enough survived to make it worthwhile.

Carved out of the mountain of rock on the island, the caves may not seem impressive after visiting Ajanta and Ellora (see p. 118), but the **Great Cave** is 40 m (130 ft) deep and 40 m wide. To the west stands Shiva's emblem.

On the rear wall is the **Shiva Mahesamurti**, a bust of Shiva as the Supreme Lord, while the angry destroyer, *Bhairava*, looks to the left and his sensuous, aspect looks to the right. In a panel to the left is **Ardhanarishvara**, Shiva as man and woman.

GOA

Time to relax, and this Portuguese colony is the perfect place for it. The beaches are superb – all the white sands and palm trees you could wish for. The cuisine makes use of the best seafood in India, and the Goans, of mixed Hindu and Portuguese descent, are a lively community of people to relax with. Still hanging on are also a few glazed-eyed latterday hippies, like relics of a bygone age.

As a change from flying down, many people like to take the more leisurely steamer from Bombay.

Embarkation takes place at the Alexandra Dock, where there are de luxe sleeping-berths for the 22-hour trip to the Goan capital city of Panaji (formerly Panjim), which will give you the oppportunity of a good look at the often dramatic mountains of the Western Ghats running parallel to the coast.

After the now world famous Vasco da Gama had landed down on the Malabar Coast in 1498, the Portuguese invaded the area and seized Goa from the Sultan of Bijapur in the year 1510. They held the colony for the next 450 years until finally Nehru launched an attack and drove them out.

Besides being a vital link for Portugal's colonial trade in the Indian Ocean, Goa became, with its succession of devout followers of different faith: the Franciscans, Augustinians, Dominicans and the Jesuits, together with a rigorous Inquisition to hold them in line, a prime base for missionary activity, most notably led by Francis Xavier who came to Goa in the year 1542. The traders have now gone but the missionaries' ancient churches in Velha Goa still stand and make a fascinating sightseeing trip – that is if you can ever manage to tear yourself away from the paradisical beaches, which are so inviting.

The most popular beaches of all are **Calangute** and **Dona Paula**, each of them within easy reach of

---

Francis Xavier's Relics

Every ten years – the next time in 1994 – the body of St. Francis Xavier is carried from the church of Bom Jesus to be exhibited at the cathedral. But not a lot of his body is left today In the year 1554 a Portuguese lady bit a toe off, another toe fell off and is kept in a crystal box, the right hand was donated to a Catholic community in Nagasaki, while other pieces were sent to Rome.

the capital, Panaji, and excursions out to Velha Goa. If you want to get away from the madding crowd, the most secluded and unspoiled white sands can be found along the incredible 40 km (25 miles) of **Colva Beach**, which run immediately south of Dabolim Airport, right down to the lovely and inviting **Benaulim** and **Betul**.

Velha Goa

The 16th-century churches to be found in Velha (or Old) Goa have been beautifully restored, but you will doubtlessly notice that, without the town buildings that used to surround them, they have acquired the strangely melancholic air of old museum-pieces.

The town once had a population of 350,000 and some 100 churches. Nowadays the laterite stonework of many of the remaining churches has been thoughtfully and carefully covered with lime plaster to protect them against deterioration from the heavy waters of the dreaded Indian monsoons which threaten to disrupt so much in everyday life.

Distinguished from others by the harmonious simplicity of its rib-vaulted nave, **St. Francis of Assisi** is the oldest church still standing in Velha Goa, perhaps dating as far back 1521. The fine arabesque and floral frescoes are the work of local Indian artists who have let themselves go on themes wholly familiar to them, in contrast with their clumsy efforts to paint portraits of the saints, with whose images they were, despite the hard work of the missionaries, perhaps not as much at home.

The Tuscan Renaissance façade of **Sé Cathedral**, the single biggest Christian church in India, has a certain elegance to it despite a loss of symmetry since its north tower collapsed in 1776. The enormous main altar, which is dedicated to St. Catherine of Alexandria, shows in a series of sumptuously gilded panels some scenes from the saint's martyrdom.

Sandstone and granite were the materials used to build the Baroque church of **Bom Jesus**, famous for it's casket of St. Francis Xavier's relics in the mausoleum to the right of the altar. The mausoleum was designed in Florence, as a gift from the Grand Duke of Tuscany.

The Arabian Sea off the coast of Goa, a moment to dream.

THE CENTRE

Here you touch the very soul of India, at the holy city of Varanasi and the Ganga, and its sensuality in the many temples of Khajuraho. There's also a strong reminder of the historic reality of the Indian Mutiny at Lucknow, You can also escape the preoccupations of man at the wildlife sanctuary of Kanha.

LUCKNOW

As a logical stop-over on your way to Varanasi (coming from Delhi or from Calcutta), Lucknow is worth a visit for its special place in the history of India's determined fight for Independence – a focus of the Mutiny of 1857 (see p. 37-39).

The **British Residency** – today preserved as a monument – initially commemorated British resistance, but since Independence it has been visited by Indians interested in this relic of their own struggle for self-assertion – and for a family picnic on the lawns.

On a lawn surrounded by 24 palm trees, a cenotaph pays tribute to Chief Commissioner Sir Henry Lawrence, who was killed during the attack. An obelisk here honours 'Native Officers and Sepoys, who died...nobly performing their duty'. Indians constituted half the 1,600 troops defending the Residency.

A little **museum** inside tells the history of the siege with a model of the first Residency, as well as rusty cannons and cannonballs, prints, photos and letters.

Down by the river, a short walk away, is the **Martyrs' Memorial**, inaugurated in 1957 on the centenary of the Mutiny, to honour the fighters for India's independence.

Lucknow used to be a Moslem stronghold and although the size of its community has now dwindled to only 30 percent of the country's population, it is one of the two single most important Indian centres of Shiite doctrine, the other being Bombay. However, its 18th- and 19th-century mosques, are without architectural distinction.

VARANASI

One thing is certain: you cannot begin to fathom the mystery of India without a visit to Varanasi. Not that this old city will 'explain' everything – in fact, its dramatic confrontations of life and death on the Ganga river, of scholarship and superstition, may only mystify you even further – but the city's aura of sanctity is so overwhelming that it supercedes any need for rational explanations.

Perhaps the Moslem conquerors perceived the Hindus' reverence for Varanasi as a threat – there is no temple in this 3,000-year-old city dating back beyond the 18th century – but it became a holy city for Moslems, too, with Emperor Aurangzeb even trying to rename it Muhammadabad.

The name Varanasi, misheard as by Europeans as Benares, comes from its site between the tributaries of the life-giving holy river Ganga, the Varuna and Asi. Shiva is said to have poured the river down on the plains from the Himalayas, and it is for reasons of this mythical story leads Hindus to see it as the oldest city in the world.

Probably founded by the Indo-Aryans around 1000 BC – it was established from earliest times as a famous seat of learning for Hindu thinkers: theologians, philosophers and poets alike. It has remained ever since an outstanding centre of the Hindu sciences.

It was just outside Varanasi that Buddha's disciples gathered in the 6th-century BC to hear his sermon at the Deer Park of Sarnath. Since then, Jain monks, Moslems and Sikhs, have proclaimed it a holy city and have built monasteries, mosques and temples here.

The Ghats

These stone-stepped embankments leading down to the Ganga river are the gathering place of more than 250,000 pilgrims a year. To see the day unfold at the Ghats, you must rise before dawn to join the pilgrims. Holy men and women are up and about, busily chanting *'Ganga Mai ki jai!'* – 'Praise be to Mother Ganga!'

Some are *sannyasi*, wandering beggars who have abandoned their homes and walked all the way from Madras to stand on the Ghats and pray, to bathe and drink the waters of the holy river or just to sit and meditate this supreme moment of their religious lives.

Even the most aged and infirm travel here to die, for nothing is more blessed for a devout Hindu than to die in the great waters of the Varanasi and thus be released from the eternal cycle of rebirth.

The rising sun on the ghats of the Ganga, the faithful come to pray.

All roads in town seem to lead down to the **Dasaswamedh Ghat,** where Brahma the Creator is said to have made a ritual sacrifice of 10 horses. At the top of the steps, the holy men sit under their bamboo umbrellas, chanting *mantras*, and offering, for a coin or grains of rice, either sandalwood paste, flowers and water from the Ganga.

At the water's edge, you can rent a boat and go into midstream for a view of the impressive skyline featuring many Hindu temples, *gopuram* towers, Moslem minarets and Mughal domes.

In the 5 km (3 miles) between her tributaries, the Ganga describes a crescent, turning north, as it is suggested, for one last gesture of farewell to her sacred home in the Himalayas before descending east towards the Bay of Bengal. You can ask your boatman to take you further upstream, to the Asi Ghat before doubling back as far as the Panchganga.

Notice how the ritual ablutions, which are highly elaborate when performed by a learned Brahman,

Sports, Sacred and Secular

With the aid of a small mirror and a graceful arching hand gesture consecrated in temple sculpture all over India, pilgrims use white paste to daub a tilak *or* tika *mark on their forehead, made up of a dots, stripes or triangles, which denote their sect, according to whether they are adepts of Vishnu or Shiva.*

Women apply a red parting to denote their married status. Many Indian women, wherther married or unmarried, wear the red spot or tika *these days in any colour, simply as a cosmetic accessory.*

usually involve a kind of crouching movement completed at least three times in the water. Women, you will notice, bathe in full sari.

You'll see plenty of less ritual soap and shampoo and, on the **Dhobi Ghat**, laundry-washing, too – Mother Ganga is sacred, but also just a river. Out on stone platforms, young men perform gymnastics, which form part of a devout self-discipline known as *danda*.

Those people who might at first be reluctant to confront the omni-presence of death along the river will be impressed by the simple dignity of the funeral rites here.

Families bring their dead for their cremation to the holiest of Varanasi ghats, **Manikarnika**.

The body, in a white shroud, is carried on a bier of bamboo to the river's edge, where a few drops of Ganga water are poured into the lips of the dead. The body is placed on a pyre of perfumed sandalwood, which is then set alight.

At **Man Mandir Ghat** is Jai Singh's observatory, the **Scindia Ghat**, with its leaning temple. The Alamgir Mosque rises behind the sacred **Panchganga Ghat**, said to be the mythical confluence of four Ganga subterranean tributaries.

The Town

The **Chawk** (bazaar) is famous for its perfumes, silks and brassware.

Look out for the gilded **Golden Temple of Vishwanath**, the holiest temple of Varanasi, forbidden to non-Hindus. You can view it from the building opposite, before going behind the temple to see the sacred bull, stained deep vermilion by the libations of its worshippers.

The Varanasi Hindu University has an **Art Museum** with a superb collection of 16th-century Mughal miniatures, considered superior to the national collection in Delhi.

Sarnath

Now a suburb of Varanasi, which is located about 10 km (6 miles) out of town, Sarnath is where Buddha gave his famous Deer Park sermon to five disciples around the year 530 BC, the veritable foundation of the religion (see p. 54-55).

It quickly became, as it still is today, a leading pilgrimage site, attracting devout Buddhists from many Eastern countries including Japan, China and South-east Asia.

Emperor Ashoka commanded his edict-pillars to be built within the monasteries and stupas, which he had ordered to be built in their thousands, but just like Varanasi, Sarnath suffered at the hands of Qutb-ud-din in the year 1194.

Today the ruins have been well restored, and are accompanied by an excellent museum of Buddhist sculpture, which you should save to enjoy until last.

On the western side of the road coming out of Varanasi, you'll find the **Chaukhaudi Stupa**, built by a Gupta king in the 5th century AD. With a proud octagonal tower that rises out of the top of the structure, it was built to mark the passage of the Emperor Humayun after his defeat in the 1540s.

Not By Faith Alone

It is hard to convince the faithful that the Ganga river is not pure. For centuries, those people not permitted for religious reasons to be cremated on the ghats – which included babies and victims of cholera – have been dropped in the river while people bathe in and drink the water nearby.

Many firmly believe that the Ganga grants self-purification, which is reinforced for some by chemical analyses revealing an 0.05 percent sulphur content to conquer the bacteria. While faith has provided many bathers with a strong psychosomatic weapon against contamination, many of the people living permanently by the Varanasi ghats suffer from gastro-intestinal diseases.

To combat Ganga's pollution of dead bodies, sewage and raw industrial waste, a $250 million campaign is finally under way. For the Indian government, faith needs a little help.

In a pretty setting of flowers and sacred neem trees, the remains of seven redbrick **monasteries** dating from the 3rd-century BC to the 9th century can be discerned among the ruins.

Since its attractive bricks were carried off to build houses in the town, only a platform remains of the **Main Shrine** itself, which once marked Buddha's dwelling place during his stay at Sarnath.

West of the shrine, surrounded by an iron railing, are the stump and fragments of **Ashoka's Pillar**, which was once over 15 m (48 ft) high. Notice how the shine of the granite has withstood the elements for over 2,200 years.

Its inscription warns the Indian people against the dissidence that could upset the important national unity under his leadership: 'No one shall cause division in the Order of Monks.'

The dominant feature of these ruins is the 45-metre (146-ft) high cylindrical **Dhamekh Stupa** which was built in the 5th century AD and which is believed by many to mark the ancient site of Buddha's most famous sermon.

Immediately below eight empty niches – perhaps they once held the statues on display in the museum – is a beautifu frieze of fine floral and geometrical patterns, interspersed with pretty birds and small seated Buddhas. If you should have a pair of binoculars, this is when they come in handy: take a close look at the fine craftsmanship which is reflected in this work of art.

Visitors will take delight in the **Museum**, which is a treasure-trove of superb early Indian sculpture dating from the 3rd-century BC to the 5th century AD.

Greeting you as you enter the museum is its famous masterpiece, the **lion-capital** of Ashoka's pillar, a high point of the distinctive art of the Mauryan empire.

With its power and pride it was an understandable choice as the emblem of India's regained nationhood in 1947. Four vigorous lions stand, back to back, atop a frieze of animals comprising a horse, an elephant, a bull and a smaller lion, each of them separated by a Wheel of Law, resting on an inverted lotus that once connected it to the pillar.

Against the wall is the **Wheel of Law** that originally rose above the lions. As a gentle counterpoint to this, and sculpted some 700 years later, a **cross-legged Buddha** with a finely chiselled halo was added. Look out for it.

The Deer Park to the north of the excavations is just a modern afterthought, pleasant to relax in, but not related to the original.

KHAJURAHO

This town is famous for the erotic sculptures of its medieval Hindu temples, and many come expecting to snigger. They leave, however, with sighs of admiration because the sandstone temples are marvels of harmony and the sculptures have true grace in their sensuality that stifles any temptation to smirk.

We have the British hunters to thank for uncovering these masterpieces, around 1840, half-buried in earth and overgrown by the jungle. They didn't see the light of day until their excavation in 1923, 600 years after being abandoned during the Moslem conquests.

Khajuraho was capital of the Rajput kingdom of the Chandellas, a clan that brought vigour to love and war, as is clear in the temples they built from the 10th to the 12th centuries.

The temples are divided into three groups, western, eastern and southern. The major ones, in the western group, are in a beautifully kept park with paths leading you easily from one to the other. To see the sculptures at their best, go in the morning or afternoon, or both, and then go back at night, when the temples are illuminated.

The lovely **Lakshmana** temple dedicated to Vishnu, is one of the earliest of all and the only one to have preserved its four shrines at each corner of the square platform on which it stands.

Four *sikhara* domes rise above the entrance-porch, the *mandapa* hall for worshippers, a larger hall for dancing-girls, and the inner sanctuary, surrounded by an ambulatory for walking round the image of the deity. The silhouette seems to suggest the Himalayan home of the gods, but this may be more of a Brahmanic interpretation than the conception of the architect.

The sculptures portray not only erotic postures, but also the adventures of Krishna: in one he uses all four arms to fend off two wrestlers.

Visvanartha, built in 1002, is more compact and ultimately more harmonious than Lakshmana. Its sculptures include a flute-playing maiden and a small nymph pulling a thorn from her foot.

The most spectacular temple of the western group is **Kandariya-Mahadeva**, with its three domes culminating in the great 30-metre-high (98-ft) *sikhara*, composed of row upon row of other smaller *sikharas*, 84 in all.

KHAJURAHO

Created at the height of the Chandellas' power, in the mid-11th century, the sculpture in it is the most sophisticated and ingenious – *apsara* dancing-girls, *sura-sundari* nymphs coquettishly yawning or scratching, applying their make-up, playing with monkeys or parakeets or with their cheerful lovers. The Kandariya is the largest of all the Khajuraho temples and adds, with its grand scale, a special exuberance to the life-enhancing spirit of the place. Only the wettest of wet blankets would seriously suggest this was decadent.

The eastern group of structures includes three Jain temples. The most important is the 10th-century **Parsvanatha**, which was built in the classical Hindu *sikhara*-domed style and incorporating the sculptural themes of the Vishnu temples. While the religion of the Jains stops short here of anything too explicit in sexuality, the ambience is clearly contagious and there are obviously a lot of voluptuous, full-breasted ladies you don't usually see on a Jain temple.

Khajuraho raises sexual agility to the realm of high art.

140

KANHA

Kanha is famous and it is widely acknowledged as the best place for seeing an Indian tiger in the wild. In fact, from the point of view of the sheer abundance of wildlife to be seen here, Kanha is probably the best national park in India and so should not be missed.

You might think the journey is a little complicated, but if you go to the trouble you will find it well worth the effort. Either you can fly into Nagpur or, if you're coming from Khajuraho, take a train to Jabalpur, and continue by road. It is, however, best to reserve your accommodation in the forest rest-houses in advance of your journey.

The best season is February to May, when you'll be able to see plenty of beautiful cheetal (spotted deer), blackbuck, sloth bear, gaur or bison (largest of the wild cattle), wild boar, Kanha's unique barasingha ('12-pointer') swamp deer and also monkeys galore.

The 'Project Tiger' campaign is doing a sterling job here to protect the king of India's jungles, without neglecting that elusive animal: the leopard. Enthusiastic bird-watchers might also spot black ibis and the crested serpent-eagle.

Tracking down the tiger is a subtle affair, and requires a degree of dedication married with calm and secrecy.

On your first morning you take a jeep-safari at dawn to scout the terrain. The forest of sal trees and bamboo is a truly sweet-smelling delight, interspersed with rolling green meadows where the deer and gaur graze. Game trackers will be out by this time in an attempt to locate the tiger's hunting ground for the evening safari.

Elephants with a team of jungle-wise mahouts set out in the afternoon to seek the tiger in what are thought to be the most likely areas, and you will be following in a jeep in a combined operation, keeping alert for any tell-tale signs that will tell you the tiger is near.

The kind of things to listen and look out for could be any one, or perhaps several, of the following: the alarm bark of the deer, a noisy screech from the monkeys; and the most sign of all, vultures waiting for the tiger to abandon the leftovers of what he caught for lunch. When the elephant has located a tiger, the mahout signals and you hop aboard his howdah to penetrate the jungle. *Et voilà!*

SANCHI

About one hour away from Bhopal, the stupas of Sanchi are the most admired Buddhist monuments in the whole of India.

The site is on a 91 m (300 ft) hill on the Vindhya plateau, from the 3rd century BC, when Emperor Ashoka ordered stupas containing the Buddha's relics to be built.

Stupas were originally burial mounds, and Buddhism developed them as shrines of plaster-covered stone, inside it a casket containing relics of Buddha. Crowned by a *chhattra* (umbrella) made of stone, the stupa was erected on a terrace with a fence to enclose the path.

The stupas of Sanchi lay in the jungle until they were uncovered by the British in 1818, but delay in their restoration led to them being plundered. Three stupas and the temples and monasteries from the 5th to the 12th century AD can still be seen..

The **Great Stupa**, Stupa I, built in the 1st century BC, envelops a smaller mound erected nearly 200 years earlier. It is surrounded by stone railings.

In the terrace railing are four *torana* gates, off north-south and east-west axes, perhaps in order to deceive evil spirits. Formed by square posts with finely sculptured panels, topped by three architraves (crossbars), one placed above the other with dwarfs or animals.

At this time Buddha himself is not represented in human form, but symbolized by the horse on which he rode away from his palace, by the wheel of law, by his footprints, and by the pipal tree under which he found enlightenment.

The rest of humanity is present in his worshippers, his adversaries, dancers and *yaksi* nymphs. Despite the strict asceticism preached by Buddhism, it's clear that the craftsmen employed were given free rein for their joyous sensuality.

The smaller **Stupa III**, to the north-east of the Great Stupa, has one *torana* gate, and was originally built to contain the relics of the two disciples of Buddha, preserved in a casket with pieces of bone and jewels. The mound of **Stupa II** is down on the western slope of the hill. Its circular balustrade with four L-shaped entrances with its simpler decoration of flora, fauna and Buddha-symbols. Historians have noted that the horsemen are using stirrups, the earliest known example of their use in India.

THE EAST

The east of India encompasses the birthplace of Buddhism at Bodh Gaya, the great Hindu temples of Bhubaneshwar, and the challenge of Calcutta, a huge confrontation of vitality and hardship. You can cool off in the green tea-plantations of Darjeeling or in the mountains of Sikkim.

CALCUTTA

The town's reputation for squalor has so deeply imbedded itself in the world's imagination that it comes as a surprise to find the Calcuttans to be the liveliest bunch of people in the country.

Bengalis are irrepressible, and the challenge of just coping with daily life in this city of 10 millions has sharpened their wit so that an alert visitor will be fascinated and even in the end, yes, entertained.

Survival here is a creative art and it is no accident that Calcutta remains the country's intellectual and cultural capital long after it had relinquished government to Delhi. Calcutta was the home of the writer Rabindranath Tagore, India's first Nobel Prize winner, and home of the philosophers Ramakrishna and Vivekananda. Creative people still make their national name here.

After the establishment-minded press of Delhi, the newspapers in Calcutta seem bright, ebullient and vitriolic, and while Bombay's film-makers are masters of melodrama, Calcutta's cinema is known for its sensitivity and poetry, producing faithful mirrors of village and city life in the hands of such directors as Satyajit Ray and Mrinal Sen. It is the proper home for the country's best museum, which is simply and aptly named 'the Indian Museum'.

For all their ardent nationalism, Calcuttans retain a strong, if sometimes sardonic attachment to things British, in particular they have an affection for the English language which you'll find spoken here with the most British of accents and often with a good deal more style and elegance than the British themselves can muster.

The West Bank

Even if you're not arriving in the city by train, start your visit over at **Howrah Station**. The crowds in and around the station will give you something of a baptism by fire, and you'll soon realize that only a small fraction of them are actually there to take a train. For many the station is a home, its entrance-hall and platforms are a dormitory – and a kitchen.

Aim for the restful **Botanical Gardens**, which were laid out in the 18th century, boasting 35,000 species of flowers and shrubs. It was here that the first tea cuttings were brought here from China to found the plantations of Darjeeling (see p. 155-156) and Assam.

The gardens' pride is the 200-year-old banyan tree, the *Ficus bengalensis* or strangling fig tree. Some fungus disease destroyed its central trunk, but it still thrives with a circumference of 400 metres (1,300 ft.), having aerial roots.

The **Howrah Bridge** takes you across the river to the city centre and is a national monument. This massive steel suspension bridge stages the most magnificent traffic jams. It is a great place to gauge the Bengali temperament.

The City

In the centre of the city is another park, the **Maidan**, landscaped to create a clear line of fire all round from **Fort William**, and rebuilt by Robert Clive on a more defensible site than its predecessor.

Like Britain's Hyde Park, the Maidan attracts ferocious soap-box orators predicting the end of the world, but also the most wonderful charlatans peddling medicine and smoking weed, and equally dodgy tea and snacks.

The **Ochterlony Monument** is named after some obscure British warrior and one of many Calcutta landmarks taking a long time to get used to its new name (Shahid Minar). It is the focus of the city's boisterous political rallies.

By the river is **Eden Gardens**, with pond and pagoda, and the venerable Calcutta cricket grounds.

The **Victoria Memorial** offers a history of the bygone Raj, Anglo-Renaissance in style with a touch of the Mughals. Its white marble was brought from the Rajasthani quarries used for building the Taj Mahal's. It was commissioned by Viceroy Lord Curzon and paid for by 'voluntary contribution' of the maharajas and nawabs.

CALCUTTA

Toehold on the Hooghly

When the body of Shiva's wife, Kali, was dismembered after her death, the little toe of her right foot fell onto the bank of the Hooghly river and that's where the village of Kalikata grew up. Together with the other villages of Sutanuti and Govindpur it was sold to the East India Company in the 1690s to set up the trading counter of Calcutta.

It was the Nawab of Bengal's attack on the British settlement in 1756 that brought Robert Clive's crushing reprisal at Plassey and the consolidation of the British Empire in India. Calcutta, with its port-connection to east Asia and subsequent development of jute, cotton, silk and tea, remained its capital for the next 150 years. The Bengalis and Calcuttans in particular were trouble-makers, however, violently stirred by the growing nationalism. The British found it wise to move the political capital to Delhi in 1911.

Ever since Independence, when Partition cut Calcutta's jute and other industries off from their natural hinterland in eastern Bengal, the city has had its many economic difficulties compounded by a huge influx of refugees from Bangladesh. The town remains a hotbed of active, radical politics, and a stronghold of the Indian Communist Party.

Catch up on the Indian avant-garde – and the Bohemian people of Calcutta – at the **Academy of Fine Arts** on the south-east corner of the Maidan.

Running along the eastern edge of the Maidan, the **Chowringhee Road** (Nehru Road) marks the old European neighbourhood whose mansions once won Calcutta the wishful name of 'City of Palaces'. Nowadays it is a busy shopping street, with big hotels and cinemas, gigantic film billboards featuring actresses in wet saris, and a roadway that is so chock-a-block with cows, rickshaws, pedestrians and bicycles that cars are often seen going backwards.

By Chowringhee and Sudder Street, the **Indian Museum** makes an excellent home for art treasures from the ancient Maurya and Gupta eras that had been disintegrating after centuries of exposure to the merciless natural elements. In its **Bharhut Gallery** it has preserved the great Buddhist carvings on the railings from the Bharhut stupa (2nd century BC), comparable to those of Sanchi (see p. 143). The **Gandhara Room** has the earliest sculptures representing Buddha in human form (1st century AD).

In **Dalhousie Square** (also called BBD Bagh), on the site of the original Fort William north of the Maidan, was once the centre of Britain's imperial bureaucracy. Here, scribblers of the East India Company – *babus* to friend and foe – duplicated and triplicated everything they could lay their hands on, in the Writers' Buildings. It now serves just the Government of West Bengal, but with an undiminished number of *babus*.

It takes a detective to find the original site of the **Black Hole**, at the domed General Post Office on the west side of Dalhousie Square, since most Indians aren't interested in helping you. They generally see the incident (see p. 35) as having been a piece of elaborate British propaganda thought up to justify Clive's retaliation. A plaque marks the spot in an arch at the north-east corner of the post office.

Most of the major British Indian buildings prior to the 20th century were built not by an architect but by a soldier-engineer copying a set of already existing plans buildings back home.

The magnificent **Raj Bhavan** (Governor's Residence) which you can find due north of the Maidan, copied famous Kedleston Hall in Derbyshire. The nearby **St. John's Church**, Calcutta's first cathedral, is an Indian version of London's St.-Martin-in-the-Fields. Look in the south aisle for John Zoffany's bemusing painting of *The Last Supper,* which used the East India Company men as models, with the painter's sworn enemy, Mr. Paull, as Judas. In the church cemetery is the tomb of Job Charnock, the Company official who founded the city of Calcutta.

A bizarre tribute to Western art and architecture can be found at the **Marble Palace** of the hugely wealthy landowning family of Raja Majendra Mullick Bahadur, in the tiny Muktaram Babu Street northeast of Dalhousie Square.

This huge Palladian villa turned museum, has a park and menagerie of exotic birds, and recalls William Randolph Hearst's Castle built in California with its imaginative, not to say wild juxtaposition of ancient Roman and Chinese sculpture, fine Venetian glass chandeliers, Sèvres porcelain, old Flemish masters and naughty French erotica. The odd Mullick still hangs around to play Chopin in the ballroom or billiards in the parlour.

149

BHUBANESHWAR

As you fly down the coast from Calcutta, you'll suddenly spot a veritable small forest of tall domes in a town with a lake at its centre. These are the temples of that most holy city: Bhubaneshwar,

The capital of Orissa is a centre for easy day-trips to the ancient Jain cave-monasteries of Udaigiri, the chariot-temple of Konarak and sacred pilgrimage town of Puri.

Once there were thousands of Hindu and Jain sanctuaries in and around Bhubaneshwar. Some 500 can still be traced, mostly ruins, but 30 are visitable. Three or four are masterpieces of Hindu architecture.

The oldest temple (7th and 8th centuries) are grouped around the sacred 'Ocean Drop' lake of **Bindu Sagar,** the focus for bathing and purification ceremonies before the annual festivals.

East of the Bindu Sagar is the 10th-century **Muktesvara,** a rust-coloured stone temple dedicated to Shiva, with its small bathing tank and gracefully arched *torana* gate.

Like their sisters in Europe, the gypsies of India make wonderful use of jewellery.

There is great peace and dignity in the temple's proportions. The low curved pyramid on the hall of worship and ribbed *sikhara* dome over the sanctum shows the classic silhouette of Orissa temples.

The **Rajarani**, standing on a platform at the end of a pleasant garden, is a more robust structure than that of the Muktesvara, and

has a more pronounced pyramid over the worship-hall and powerful *sikhara* behind it.

 The greatest of the city's many temples is the **Lingaraja** late 11th century, south of the Bindu Sagar. Off limits to non-Hindus, it can be viewed from an observation platform, which was specially erected for the purpose by Lord Curzon.

You'll find a pair of binoculars will come particularly useful here for appreciating the splendid detail of the carving on the soaring central tower dominating what is a whole complex of temples. It is dedicated to the Lord of the Three Worlds, Tribhuvanesvara, which gave the town of Bhubaneshwar its modern day name.

Udaigiri

The cave-monasteries of Udaigiri are close to Bhubaneshwar airport.

Excavated from a sandstone hill in the 3rd and 2nd centuries BC, the Udaigiri (Sunrise Hill) caves were dwellings for priests and monks when Jainism was the state religion in the kingdom of Kalinga.

Rani's Monastery (Cave 1) has carvings of elephants, maidens and court dancers, but unlike the caves of Ajanta and Ellora (see p. 119), there are no temples or central halls for worship.

Further up the hill, **Ganesha Gumpha** (Cave 10) is set back on an esplanade and guarded by two sturdy stone elephants on the porch holding branches of mangoes. The friezes are more sophisticated and show archers riding elephants and a king of Kalinga reclining with his queen. Cave 14, **Hathi Gumpha** (Elephant Cave), is important for the inscription above the entrance, which details King Kharavela's conquests and irrigation projects completed during his 13-year reign around 50 BC.

Konarak

The **Sun Temple** of Konarak was conceived as a gigantic chariot for the great sun-god Surya cantering inland from the Indian Ocean.

The *sikhara* that once towered 60 m (200 ft) into the air, like some symbolic and divine charioteer, has gone, but the grandiose pyramid of the **Jagmohan** (Hall of Audience), where the priests used to officiate, still soars above 12 pairs of huge stone wheels sculpted into its huge platform and drawn by numerous galloping horses.

The temple was built in the 13th century, but the *sikhara* toppled, its porous stone a victim of storms and plunderers – and of the ambitious concept of its architect. As you climb over the remains, you'll find it has a decidedly secular air.

Surya was given his due with dignified green chlorite statues of *parsva-devatas* (sun-deities) set in niches facing the four points of the

The sun-god's giant stone temple chariot has ground to a halt.

compass and with the emphasis of much of the sculpture profusely decorating the walls placed on the life of the king – his battles, the royal hunt and life at court. The sensuality of the aristocratic lovers recalls Khajuraho (see p. 139).

(see p. 139)

Wheel of Life

Jagannath, the Universal Lord, is an incarnation of Vishnu the Preserver, offering Hindus of all castes the opportunity to escape the torment of perpetual rebirth. Therefore thousands of pilgrims converge on Puri all year round, but mostly for the June festival when the three great wooden chariots of Jagannath and his brother and sister are drawn through the streets. Then, the faithful can liberate themselves by touching the crudely carved wooden deities, models of which are sold in the town.

Although orthodox followers of Vishnu insist that Jagannath is a life-giving force, the belief still persists that the frenzied activity of the festival has led some to seek the ultimate release by hurling themselves under the huge wheels of the Jagannath, whence the English word 'juggernaut', which means a great force demanding utter self-sacrifice.

The wheels of the chariot themselves, symbols of the Hindu cycle of rebirth, have beautifully carved spokes and hubs decorated with kings and gods. Beneath the wheels you can find lively carved friezes of elephants playing with children. Look out, too, for a giraffe, which indicates the Indian west coast's early contact with Africa.

The masterpieces among the free-standing statuary, though, are the war-horses trampling the king's enemies and the splendid elephants crushing the demons.

European sailors, for whom the temple was an important landmark enabling them to keep out of the dangerous shallows of the Orissa coast, called it the Black Pagoda – in order to be able to distinguish it from the 'White Pagoda' of Puri's whitewashed Jagannath Temple which was further down the coast – and as a result they nearly had it turned into a lighthouse.

After the huge *sikhara* tower had collapsed, however, the British saved the pyramidal Jagmohan by pouring concrete into its core, and now the Archaeological Survey of India are heroically performing massive restoration work on the important sculpture.

Puri

Even if you can't be in Puri for the tremendous Rath Yatra Festival in June, the town is worth a visit to see the phenomenon of a community devoted almost entirely to the 'industry' of its great **Temple of Jagannath**, either directly or by trading with the pilgrims.

Non-Hindus are not permitted within the temple precincts, but you can get a good **view** from the roof of the Raghunandan Library near the temple wall. Some 6,000 priests, artisans and other workers are employed within the grounds. Of the four main buildings, all of them whitewashed and decorated with bright, painted sculptures, the first is where the worshippers bring offerings of flowers and fruit, the second is for sacred dances, and the third for viewing the divine effigies, which are enshrined in the sanctum of the fourth and tallest edifice.

Puri also has a beautiful **beach**, south-west of town, which is ideal for cooling off – but those aren't sandcastles the Indians are making, they're miniature temples, for this is the **Swarga Dwara** (Heaven's Gateway) where the faithful wash away their sins.

DARJEELING

Before you overdose on the countless temples or even just on the heat of the plains, follow the wise example of the long gone British of Calcutta and get up into the hills and greenery leading to the lush cool of the celebrated tea gardens of Darjeeling.

> **Permits for Darjeeling and Sikkim**
>
> *Being so close to the militarily sensitive border-areas of Chinese Tibet, both Darjeeling and Sikkim require permits (free). Darjeeling is easy: either you obtain it automatically at the Indian Embassy at home when you get your visa or, if you're flying to Bagdogra, the closest airport, your passport will be stamped right there. You'll need a special permit for trekking beyond Darjeeling, but it's no trouble.*
>
> *A permit for Sikkim, extendable for a limited period, should be requested via an Indian Embassy, at least four weeks prior to your departure from home and picked up at the Deputy Commissioner's Office in Darjeeling. In theory the permits are also issued at the Ministry of Home Affairs in Delhi, but the red tape is bad.*

DARJEELING

At 2,185 metres (7,100 ft), you catch your breath in the rarefied air, but take in the splendour of the Himalayan mountains – mount Kanchenjunga situated in Sikkim (see p. 160) and, if you're lucky on a clear day in April and May or in late September and October, Mount Everest itself, up in Nepal.

In the year 1835, the raja of the then independent kingdom of Sikkim was pressured into ceding Darjeeling to the British. They had spied it as a healthy place for their soldiers and East India Company employees to recover from the ills of the plains, but above all also as strategically useful for controlling a pass into much-contested Nepal. With tea from seeds smuggled out of China and an influx of plantation labour from Nepal, the little village of 100 souls grew by 1849 to a community of 10,000.

Nowadays Darjeeling is part of West Bengal, but Nepali remains the official language and most people are physically of Nepalese and Tibetan origin. Buddhists account for 18 percent of the population.

A major part of the pleasure of Darjeeling is the journey. Although you're driving along narrow mountain-roads, you'll feel much safer

than in the plains because everyone takes infinitely more care, lorry and bus drivers clearly subdued by the deep ravines.

But the best way to travel up – at least part of the way if you're too impatient to take 6 hours for the whole 80 km (50 miles) – is by the **Darjeeling Himalayan Railway**, more popularly and humorously known as the 'Toy Train', which

starts out at Siliguri, not far from Bagdogra. Built in 1881, the tiny steam-train on a 60-cm (2-ft) track climbs, loops and zigzags through dense forests of sal, Chinese cedar and teak, alive with jungle birds and mountain streams.

Look out for Pagla Jhora, the Mad Torrent, just after Gayabari Station, Gladstone's Rock, like the statesman's head, near Mahanadi,

India shares its tallest mountain, Kanchenjunga, with Nepal.

and a first view of Kanchenjunga, 8,586 m (28,168 ft.) high and the world's third highest peak, (after Mount Everest and Pakistan's K2).

The railway-builders admitted it might have been safer to dig some tunnels, but they preferred

157

to go 'round the mountain' to give you a better view of the terraced tea gardens and the valleys plunging deeply down to the Bengal plains. Certainly when you reach the railway's high point, 2,257 m (7,407 ft.) at **Ghoom**, the view as you hover out on the loop over Darjeeling is in every sense of the word breathtaking.

The only relics of the British Raj are the now all-Indian and still very private Darjeeling Club (but a planter might sneak you in) and a couple of tea-rooms and Edwardian hotels like the Windermere (with coal-burning fires and hot water bottles at night).

The real British legacy is in the **tea gardens**, all Indian-run, which offer a beautiful green setting for the town and an insight into the growing and processing of the tea before it gets to you (see p. 209). Among those which are open for visitors, without obligation to buy, are Makaibari and Happy Valley. Your hotel will book for you.

It's a popular excursion to drive to **Tiger Hill** before dawn, which

Preparing a winter wardrobe in the ancient kingdom of Sikkim.

Indians and Westerners go on for different reasons, though both with an almost religious excitement as the night fades. From an observation platform, you can get a terrific view, away to the north, of Mount Kanchenjunga and, on a good day, just a small jagged peak in the distance – yes, Mount Everest. But you'll notice the Indians are facing east. What matters is not the rare opportunity of seeing the world's tallest mountain, but the *sunrise*.

For a closer look at the true roof of the world, consider a seven-day camping trek, on foot or pony, to **Sandakhpu** (3,650 m, 11,700 ft). You'll get better views of Mount Kanchenjunga and Mount Everest, and you pass through lovely forests of chestnut, magnolia, and rhododendron. During April and May, the orchids will be in bloom.

Armchair mountaineers invariably enjoy the excellent museum at the **Himalayan Mountaineering Institute** in Darjeeling, which has some fascinating memorabilia of Himalayan expeditions, particular the equipment used by local boy Sherpa Tensing Norgay, here Indianized as Shri Tensingh, when, with Edmund Hillary, he was the first to conquer Everest in 1953.

SIKKIM

Once again, a great part of the joy is the journey itself, going by road to the capital, **Gangtok** (1,768 m; 5,800 ft) in eastern Sikkim through the most spectacular scenery with rivers roaring through gorges, deep valleys outlined by terraced rice paddies, and forested hills.

To protect India's border with China and put an end to the unrest over the **Raja's** autocratic rule, the region of Sikkim was incorporated into the Indian Union in 1975. The people of Sikkim are mostly made up of Nepalese and Lepchas – the country's original settlers known also as Rongpan, the people of the ravines – and Bhutias from Tibet.

The colourful Tibetan Buddhist monasteries are the most attractive sight in the valleys near Gangtok, the most easily accessible of them being **Rumtek** which was built in the year 1968 after China drove the marroon-robed Tibetan monks of the Karmapa sect into exile.

Other, older monasteries, from the 18th century, at **Pemayangtse** and **Tashiding**, are based 150 km (92 miles) west of Gangtok, and are well worth visiting, but access to them may be restricted at times by the military authorities.

PATNA

The capital of Bihar serves as a base for seeing the sanctuaries of Bodh Gaya, Rajgir and Nalanda, but its bazaars, first-class sculpture museum, a major Sikh temple and the views of the Ganga river make it worth at least a day of your time.

Patna was already in existence 2,500 years ago, when Buddha and Mahavira, were active here. It later became the capital of the Mauryan emperors, in the 3rd century BC, and one of the largest cities in the world, 3 km (2 miles) across and 12 km (7 miles) along the Ganga.

In the 19th century, the British used Patna for manufacturing and distributing opium to keep China supplied with its favourite drug. The old warehouses can still be seen by the river in the Gulzarbagh district, now a printing press.

The **Golghar** on the west side of town near the river, is evidence of the more altruistic side of British activity in Patna. This great flat-topped dome, a granary some 27 m (87 ft) high, was erected in 1786 by Captain John Garstin 'for the perpetual prevention of famine', after the terrible famine of 1770. Climb to the top for a fine **view** of the town and river.

On the edge of the **Maidan** is the open ground where Mahatma Gandhi held mass prayer-meetings.

Stand in the middle of the new **Ganga Bridge** to catch a sense of the place the river has in the lives of the Indians. It is 3 km (2 miles) wide here.

You may be unable to visit the Sikhs' Golden Temple at Amritsar, but their **Har Mandir Takht** in old Patna will show this community. It is built on the birthplace of Gobind Singh (1666–1708), who called on the Sikhs to defend their faith with armed force (see p. 53). The well that served Govind Singh's house is now a marble shrine.

The sanctuary exemplifies piety and militancy. A priest will explain the the faith and show you, among the guru's relics, his cradle, shoes, and weapons. Above the sanctuary, priests and neophytes chant from the scriptures of the *Adi Grant* in a hall, now a museum to history and the tortures suffered by Sikhs.

The **bazaar** nearby sells cheap bamboo and leather goods.

Patna Museum offers Mauryan sculpture: a stone *yaksi* (symbol of fertility), a maiden and Buddhas, a four-armed *Padmapani*, and also a reclining *Avalokitesvara*.

Bodh Gaya

The site of the pipal tree or *bodhi*, the tree of wisdom where Gautama Siddhartha became the Enlightened One, Buddha, stands for one of the four great pilgrimages of his life. The others are those of his birth at Lumbini (Nepal); his first sermon at Sarnath (see p. 137); and of his death at Kushinagar. The sanctuary is just outside Gaya, south of Patna.

E.M. Forster fans can undertake their own private pilgrimage 25 km (15 miles) north, to the Barabar Caves, which were the setting for the 'Marabar incident' in Forster's famous novel *Passage to India*. As Forster himself commented, however, they have no artistic merit in themselves.

The towering structure of the **Mahabodhi Temple** built in the 6th century, evokes the *gopuram* gateways of south India. In keeping with other early Buddhist tennets, there is no figurative representation of Buddha here, but there is a large gilded statue from a later period inside, and behind the temple are the spreading branches and trunks of the sacred **Bodhi Tree**, which is said to have grown from a sapling of the first one which stood here 2,500 years ago. Pilgrims visiting the temple, reverently drape its branches with white and saffrong coloured veils. A platform marks Buddha's seat, and a set of large footprints symbolize his presence, while stone bowls mark where he walked. Where he bathed, Hindus and Buddhists still follow his example. The **museum** has stupa-railings, and the granite Buddhas date from the 9th century.

The importance of the Bodh Gaya pilgrimage is evident in the Japanese, Thai, Tibetan, Burmese and Chinese temples nearby.

The spice of a million curries, as can be seen near the University of Nalanda..

Rajgir

This ancient city is due north-east of Bodh Gaya, out on the road to Naland, and it has been holy to both the Buddhists and Jains since the 6th century BC – as Rajagriha, the capital of the Magadha kingdom, the town was frequented at different times in their lives by both Buddha and his contemporary Vardhamana Mahavira, the founder of the Jain religion.

The surrounding green hills are topped by numerous temples of both religions, the best known of them being placed on **Gridhakuta** (Vulture's Peak) where Buddha is believevdd to have converted the once fierce Mauryan warrior king Bimbisara to the peaceful doctrine of non-violence.

The Japanese have built a great white **stupa** on Rajgir's principle hill, which you can reach by aerial ropeway – a pleasant way to survey the rugged countryside.

> ### Waiting for Nirvana
> *The demons did not make it very easy for Gautama Siddhartha to achieve enlightenment. As he sat there beneath the pipal tree, for 49 days, the demons played the age-old game of 'good guy, bad guy' to get him to crack. First, they hit him with whirlwind, then tempest, flood and earthquake. He just sat there. Then the devil Mara brought in his lovely daughters, Desire, Pleasure and Passion, to seduce him with song, dance and caresses. He just sat there. They offered to make him king of the world. He just sat there until they gave up and went away.*
>
> *Buddha's ordeal was a godsend for Indian art. In early Buddhism, when it was considered to be sacrilegious to portray Buddha in human form, his torments and temptations provided sculptors with a rich alternative source for their creative imagination.*

Nalanda

In order for you to get the most out of the fascinating ruins of the great monastery and the University of Nalanda, you are recommended to use the services of a guide from the Archaeological Survey of India.

In the 3rd century BC Ashoka founded the first monastery in the town of Rajir, which became a centre of learning under the Gupta kings 600 years later. By the time the Chinese sage, Hiuen Tsang, came here in the 7th century, it was a thriving university for teaching philosophy, logic, grammar and medicine, and Buddhist theology. It also sent missionaries to spread Buddhism to Tibet and attracted scholars from China, Burma, as well as Thailand and Cambodia. It was destroyed by the Moslems at the end of the 12th century and the monks fled to Nepal and Tibet.

The **museum** has a good model of the original university and its monastery buildings, worth studying before you go out to the site. It also has a fine collection of bronzes from the 9th to the 12th centuries.

On the **excavation site**, you will see remains of dormitories, also the refectory, kitchens, baths, lecture halls, libraries and temples.

Try Cambridge, It's Easier

According to Hiuen Tsang, the University in Nalanda had 1,500 teachers and 10,000 students, all on scholarships funded by the 'endowment' of 100 villages in the area. But getting in was not a piece of cake.

Entrance examinations were exactly that – you couldn't get past the entrance of the university before answering a difficult oral question on philosophy, posed by the gate-keeper. Only ten per cent got through the gate.

THE SOUTH

Travelling between Delhi, Bombay and Calcutta, it's easy to forget that southern India exists. The attitude of northern Indians tends to be rather disparaging towards it, but a tour of the peninsula reveals a bright and cheerful people with a culture as rich and varied as their greener landscapes – the beautiful Malabar and Coromandel coasts.

The Dravidians that make up most of the southern populations don't mind being seen as different from northerners, but they don't want to be disregarded.

Archaeologists can trace their origins to the builders of the first cities, Harappa and Mohenjodaro in the Indus valley. Their religion included elements of Hinduism such as Shiva's phallic lingam and his sacred bull, Nandi, *before* the Brahmanic Indo-Aryans arrived.

Driven south, the Dravidians remained not only geographically separate, but also politically independent, impervious to the waves of foreign invaders arriving.

As Hindu bastions against the Moslems until the end of the 16th century, they were by no means united. The Hoysalas of Karnataka, the Cheras of Kerala, the Cholas, Pandyas and Pallavas of Tamil Nadu, all fought among themselves until the kingdom of Vijayanagar (Hampi in Karnataka) emerged as dominant in the 14th century.

Each of these kingdoms showed cultural vitality, exporting temple-builders, together with their spices and ivory to Burma and Malaya, Cambodia and Java. Suffering less than the north from the ravages of Moslem iconoclasts, their temples have survived in profusion and in much better condition.

Bangalore is in the vanguard of India's modernization, and Madras, though without the self-promotion of Bombay easily produces twice as many feature films as Bombay.

Karnataka's granite hills – like the stone walls of some forgotten giant's garden.

166

Madurai, Thanjavur (Tanjore), Belur and Halebid are custodians of the peninsula's ancient art treasures. The strong regional identity of the south has repeatedly foiled attempts to spread Hindu and make it the national language here. On the east coast they point out that Tamil literature is much richer than Hindi. On the west, the people of Kerala, who speaking Malayalam, boast the highest literacy rate in the country: 90 percent for the whole State, compared with 81 percent for the next highest, the district of Mizoram, and this with a national average of just over 52 percent.

Much better served by the rains, with some parts benefitting from the peninsula's two monsoons, in the summer and early winter, the south's vegetation is luxuriant and colourful.

There are coconut groves on the Malabar west coast, palmyra palms on the Coromandel east, and in between, a more barren landscape of rugged mountains and dramatic rocky outcroppings, relieved by a sudden, colourful flare of 'Flame of the Forest' trees, hibiscus or deep green jungle, as well as plentiful trickling streams, lotus-ponds and lakes covered with scarlet lilies.

BANGALORE

Modern and efficient, the capital of Karnataka is a convenient gateway to the western half of the peninsula.

Under the former British Raj, Bangalore, at an altitude of 930 m (3,000 ft), was the summer refuge for its Madras-based officials, who with their parks and greenery, had made Bangalore the 'garden city'. The spectacular growth of India's boom town in electronics, aviation, telecommunications and machine tools has noticeably changed the climate since the 1970s, today it is several degrees hotter than before.

There are still pleasant walks to be had, however, in **Cubbon Park** and in the terraced greenery of the botanical gardens of **Lal Bagh.**

Bangalore-Mysore road makes a delightful introduction to the verdant and pleasant land of the south, leading you along tributary streams of the Cauvery river, past groves of mango trees, sugar-cane fields and rice paddies, suddenly broken by a soaring mountain of solid granite, which director David Lean made the location for the fateful picnic in his film of E.M. Forster's novel *Passage to India*. You can visit Srirangapatnam and Somnathpur (p. 171) on the way.

MYSORE

The home-town of the maharajas regains a flicker of its old glory every October with the Dussehra festival, when the heir of the old rulers of Mysore State is paraded through the streets on his golden throne surrounded by gorgeously caparisoned elephants (see p. 202).

Mysore remains a pleasant, airy city, famous for its sandalwood and frangipani, jasmine and musk, an aroma different from that of burnt cowdung usual in northern towns.

The maharaja's **palace** is lit up at night, and is by day a museum. It was constructed in 1897 (after its predecessor was burned down, because the maharaja wanted to have a new one) and represents all the excesses of Mughal nostalgia and undigested Victoriana. Doors of solid silver open onto a multi-coloured, stylish décor of marble, mahogany and ivory. The highlight is the **art gallery** with its paintings of the maharajas in very British, landed-gentry poses and a glass case featuring a 'rolled gold replica of the British crown', set between a tea-kettle (bigger) and coffee-pot (smaller).

On the **Chamundi Hill**, one of the guest houses, Rajendra Vilas,

Diamonds Will Do It

If the great Mughal emperors turned to the ladies of their harems more for political intrigue and court ceremonial than for sexual adventures, the Maharajas of Mysore did not have the same priorities. One of them learned from a Chinese scholar that powdered diamonds made an ideal aphrodisiac. The eager prince promptly crushed practically all his kingdom's stock of sparklers, but the ladies were not impressed. He had more success, however, when his favourite, horrified by this destruction of what, after all, are a girl's best friend, persuaded him to let her personally prepare the powdered potion.

is now a hotel, and an excellent place to take tea, having a terrace which offers a fine view of Mysore. On your way back down, take a look at the massive black **Nandi** bull, Shiva's sacred mascot, with chains and bells that are a mixture of both real and sculpted items, hung around its neck.

Another popular sight are the **Brindavan Gardens**, in Mughal style, some 19 km (12 miles) north of Mysore, worth visiting at night when the fountains are floodlit.

169

Srirangapatnam

The names of many southern towns are longer than their main streets.

Situated due east of Mysore, Srirangapatnam was the site of the battles against the Moslem ruler Tipu Sultan in the 1790s, in which the British gained control of the peninsula.

The fort, which was taken by Lord Cornwallis and one Colonel Arthur Wellesley, (the Iron Duke with the rubber boots), no longer stands today, but the sultan's summer palace, **Darya Daulat Bagh**, has been preserved as a museum honouring the brave resistance of Tipu and his father, Haidar Ali.

Somnathpur

The **Kesava Temple** built in 1268 is a jewel of Indian architecture.

The structure is small, no more than 10 m (30 ft) high, its *vimanas* (shrines) seton a low platform, but achieves a grandeur in miniature, enclosed in its courtyard, isolated from the rest of the village.

The temple has been dedicated to Vishnu in his various aspects:

Plenty of apples each day to keep the Bangalore doctors away.

Epic Extraordinary
To understand the place in Indian culture of the Mahabharata, you must imagine the Bible combined with Homer's Iliad. With more than 90,000 stanzas, it's the world's longest poem, 15 times longer than the Bible. Besides grandiose tales of courage and treachery, romance and cunning, it also includes sacred texts such as Krishna's great sermon known as the Bhagavad Gita.

Here, with sacrilegious brevity, is the story: King Dhritarashtra is forced by blindness to give up his throne. He offers it to the Pandavas, five sons of his brother Pandu. But his own sons, the Kauravas, want the kingdom for and so drive out the Pandavas. When Dhritarashtra then seeks to reconcile the feuding claimants by dividing the kingdom between them, his sons trick the Pandavas out of their share with a game of dice and force the Pandavas into exile for 13 years.

More treachery ends with a bloody war involving all the kings of India and quite a few Greeks, Bactrians and Chinese, too. The Pandavas emerge as the victors, rule for many years in peace and glory, then renounce their throne to go on a holy pilgrimage to the Himalayas, where they enter the City of the Gods. After 90,000 stanzas, they deserve the rest.

as Janardana, the punisher, shown as a rigid, solemn-looking statue on the north *vimana*; as Kesava, the Radiant, after whom the temple is named but whose statue is missing from the central shrine; and as Venugopala, the Krishna on the south shrine, with another Krishna as cowherd listening at his feet.

With a domed *sikhara* on each shrine, the temple's overall effect remains 'horizontal' in the style of the Hoysala kingdom, emphasized by the layers of narrow, parallel carved friezes running around the walls. Not a square centimetre of the temple's surface is unsculpted. An unusual feature in the Hoysala temples is that their carvings are signed by the sculptors.

Like the statues of Romanesque and Gothic cathedrals portraying events from the Bible, the carvings are intended to be read like a book by those who had no access to the scriptures, which were at that time reserved for the Brahmans. They tell the stories of the gods, of the mischievous tricks of Krishna, as a child stealing butter from his mother and later as a young man stealing saris from girls bathing in the river, and of the adventures of the epic *Mahabharata*.

BELUR AND HALEBID

The most comfortable way to see these important Hoysala temples is to visit them on either side of an overnight stay at Hassan, 120 km (75 miles) northwest of Mysore.

The **Chenna Kesava Temple** in Belur is also dedicated to Vishnu the Radiant, but built 150 years before, in 1117. Beware, however, of the legend that all Belur, Halebid and Somnathpur temples were by the same architect.

The Belur temple's silhouette gives it an unfinished look, but it's not certain that towers or domes were ever planned. Here too, it is the sculpture rather than the form that gives the temple its impact.

The friezes bring the building to life, once again with the legends of the gods, Shiva the demon-killer, or scenes from the *Mahabharata* – Prince Arjuna shooting a fish while looking the other way. The masterpieces are the bracket figures: a huntress, girls dancing or singing, and another about to spray her lover with rose-water.

The sunflowers blare out a brassy chorus in the fields of Halebid.

By the south doorway, on a vine chiselled beside the head of a girl dancing with a demon, you can find a lizard hunting a fly.

Hoysalesvara Temple, located in Halebid 16 km (10 miles) from Belur, is dedicated to Shiva and his wife Parvati, and is the biggest of the Hoysala temples. It suffered from Moslem iconoclasts so that it's worth visiting the **museum**, too, where some of the best of its statues are now kept.

Look at the the surprisingly fine carving of the bracket figures in the dancing-hall: this was achieved by the craftsmen by working with soft steatite soapstone, which the open air subsequently hardened to the texture of granite.

SRAVANABELAGOLA

Fifty kilometres (30 miles) east of Hassan, the Vindhyagiri Hill rises 140 m (463 ft) above the plateau with, on its top, one of the most dramatic monuments in all India, the statue of **Gommatesvara.** To get to it, you must climb barefoot – the hill is holy ground – up 644 steps cut in the rock. Take it easy and you'll find it well worth while.

Erected in AD 983, the statue crowns a sanctuary erected in the village of Sravanabelagola 1,400 years before by the Digambara sect of Jains who regarded nakedness as part of the abnegation necessary to achieve true enlightenment (see p. 56). It is believed that in the 4th century BC Chanragupta converted to Jainism at Sravanabelagola and fasted to death.

Coming upon the statue at the top of the hill, even though you may have already seen it from a distance, it is still an awe-inspiring experience.

This Jain saint looms 17.5 m (57 ft) tall, carved from a granite monolith polished by centuries of libations with milk.

Gommatesvara, the son of the prophet Adinath, is entirely naked except for a single vine-creeper, which winds itself around his legs and arms. The creeper symbolizes the impassiveness he is said to have observed in this upright position of *pratimayoga,* which he adopted for one whole year in response to his brother's lust for worldly power. An anthill and serpents at his feet symbolize the mental agony that his smile shows he conquered.

COCHIN

One of the most charming towns in India, where Christians, Jews, Moslems and Hindus live in much greater harmony than they seem to manage elsewhere, Cochin makes a delightful gateway to the Malabar coast and the relaxed life of Kerala.

On a peninsula separated from the mainland by islands, the old part of the town is known as **Fort Cochin**, where Vasco da Gama set up Portugal's first Indian trading station. He was finally buried in the **Church of St. Francis**, the only Portuguese building still standing. It was subsequently converted by the Dutch to a Protestant church.

Saintly Gommatesvara is able to resist nature's many creeping irritations.

Keeping the Faith on the Malabar

The first Jews arrived here from Palestine on the Malabar coast, at nearby Cranganur, in the early centuries of the Christian era. Far from Roman persecutors, they traded peacefully with the Hindus or with Arab merchants from the Persian Gulf.

In time, their community was reinforced by new refugees from Babylon and Persia and then by others expelled from Spain and Portugal in 1492, spreading out along the coast.

As luck would have it, however, the Portuguese settled there, too, bringing their Inquisition with them and upsetting the hitherto friendly Moslems. The Jews then promptly moved to Cochin, under the protection of the local Hindu raja. The Portuguese came down from Goa to smash the synagogue in 1662, but it was restored two years later. Today, with the last community fading away, there's no kosher butcher left in Cochin, but, as they say, what's wrong with vegetarian?

The great navigator's remains were returned to Portugal in 1538 but his tombstone can still be seen on the south side of the church, set in the floor with a brass rail.

At the water's edge, on this northern tip of the peninsula, you can see in action the fishermen's beautiful **Chinese dipping nets**, a system imported from the China seas, where the fishermen would take the nets and sling them over a pyramid of four poles, which was then lowered into the water and hoisted out again by a system of rock-weights and pullies.

Hand-drawn Cochin rickshaw, vestige of a vanished colonial era.

The **Jewish quarter**, referred to as 'Jew Town', is in Mattancheri south of the fort. In the narrow streets of merchants and tailors, the Star of David, *menorah* candelabra and Jewish names are actually more plentiful than Jewish people. At Indian Independence there were a few thousand, but when the State of Israel was founded, a massive emigration left only dozens.

The **Synagogue,** with its red tabernacle and Chinese tiling, was built in 1568 . You can see the Copper Plates giving land-rights to a Jewish community on the coast back in AD 379.

177

Take a **backwaters trip** through the lagoons and around the island-villages. The local Government of India Tourist Information Office can help you hire a motor-boat with a crew.

You'll see fishermen working their dipping-nets or flinging hand-nets out with a whirling motion. On another island the women clean their shrimp at the water's edge, and you can see the ecumenical peace of a church surrounded by palm trees, with a Hindu temple on one side and a mosque on the other.

On the way back, stop off at **Bolghatty Island** in the Cochin lagoon to take tea in the elegance of the Dutch governor's mansion, now a hotel.

Wildlife enthusiasts should visit the nature reserve at **Periyar**, a drive of 194 km (120 miles) from Cochin, where elephants, bison and birds can be seen from the unique vantage point of an artificial lake. Look out for the elephants with their trunks raised like snorkels. Take two or three days – anything less is likely to be a waste of time.

KOVALAM

Trivandrum is a big town with an international airport, mostly for migrant workers going to and from the Gulf, but it's 15 km (9 miles) from the best **beaches** in India. Coconut palms, papaya, bananas, white sand and surf (beware of the strong currents) make Kovalam the ultimate in happy-go-lucky *dolce far niente*. It is not a temple, not a shrine or museum, not a palace in sight. Enjoy.

For people visiting Kashmir and who want to go on a trip down to the other end, India's southernmost point is **Cape Comorin** (two hours from Kovalam), where the Arabian Sea and Indian Ocean meet. Here there is nothing between you and Antarctica. You might see the sea's bright colours when a full moon rises at the same time that the sun is setting.

Page 178–179: Cochin inherited its dipping-nets from contacts with China. Below: no curried duck, strictly for export.

MADURAI

The ancient capital of the Pandya kings and one of the world's oldest cities, Madurai is still an important repository of Tamil culture and is today a bustling university town, Tamil Nadu's second largest after Madras.

The feverish religious activity around the 11 towering gopurams of the **Great Temple**, 17th century in its present form, gives you a sense of the intensity of Hinduism.

Its **Minakshi Devi Shrine** is dedicated to a pre-Hindu 'fish-eyed goddess' taken into the pantheon with her husband, Shiva, whose **Sundaresvara Shrine** is next to it. The Madurai festivals in April and May celebrate their marriage as a grand reconciliation with the Indo-Aryan invaders.

Enter the temple and walk to the Minakshi shrine. Since the interior of the shrines is off-limits to non-Hindus, get a view of the entire temple and the golden roofs by climbing the slippery stairs, to the top of the **south gopuram.**

Madurai's shrine to the fish-eyed goddess Minakshi is part of a veritable temple-city.

At ground level, you can see the arcaded **Golden Lotus Tank** and the temple's bathing place. At the west end of it is a detailed model of the whole temple complex.

It is busiest at the **Kambattadi Mandapa**, the ambulatory to the Sundaresvara shrine. Worshippers in procession prostrate themselves, bringing offerings of coconut and fruit, and toss tiny balls of butter onto blackened statues of Shiva. In the north-east corner is the **Hall of 1000 Pillars** (in fact only 997) with carved, bizarre lion-elephants, the heroes from the *Mahabharata,* the Pandava brothers, from whom the Madurai Pandyas claim descent.

Outside the eastern wall of the temple is the **Pudhu Mandapa**, the Hall of Audience of Tirumalai Nayak, who built the temple. It's now a bustling bazaar of tailors, metal-workers and other artisans.

Stop off at **Tirumalai's Palace**, about a kilometre south-east of the Great Temple. There you'll find an elegant relic of former splendour, with cusped arches and massive pillars modelled on the style of the great Rajput palaces of Rajasthan, but also some unmistakeably tubby Dravidian gods on a frieze running around the courtyard.

TRICHY

This is one colonial name, a short form of the equally European name Trichinopoly, that is resisting the trend to Indianization, the official name being Tiruchchirapalli, City of the Sacred Rock.

Today, it is a base for pilgrims visiting Tamil Nadu's great temple-complexes, but every school-boy, at least those from the old school, knew Trichy for the British defeats of the French there in the 1750s.

The famed **Rock Fort**, the main focus of these battles, looms over the city atop the great solid granite hill which gave the town its name. From early days the impregnable Rock served as a sanctuary, graced by temples and cave-shrines. Steep steps take you up to the Hall of a Thousand Pillars, as well as the shrine of Shiva and the Temple of Ganesh, from which there is a fine view over the Cauvery river, the towers of Srirangam and the plains beyond. Look out on the way up for the 7th-century, stout-pillared Pallava cave-shrines.

The French have maintained their presence in Trichy with the Jesuit College of St. Joseph and the adjoining red and buff neo-Gothic church of Our Lady of Lourdes.

Srirangam

The numerous temple precincts of **Sri Ranganathaswami**, set on an island formed by two arms of the Cauvery river, a few kilometres from Trichy, enclose a complete township of busy shops, booths and dwelling houses, with a population of some 60,000 people. Beyond the outside wall of the town are the temple's farmland and the coconut plantations – and a large, square lotus-covered bathing tank.

The temple itself, dedicated to Vishnu and already a theological centre by the 11th century, was founded a couple of thousand years ago – tradition takes it back to the Flood. Its present form comprises a total of seven concentric rectangular walled courts, culminating in an inner sanctum, and dates from the 15th and 16th centuries, after it had been liberated from Moslem invaders who had previously used it as a fortress, but many of the sanctuaries are in fact much older.

You enter on the south side, progress through an ornamented *gopuram* gate-tower characteristic of south Indian architecture. Pass under a series of soaring *gopurams* to witness religion as a full-time daily occupation.

The streets are crammed with vendors selling shrine-offerings of sweets, curds, coconut, as well as garlands and holy images. Elsewhere, men are cleaning the stables for the temple elephants and storehouses for the chariot-shrines that carry the deities through the streets during the festivals. Look out for the handsome pillared verandahs of the dwelling-houses.

Non-Hindus are allowed as far as the fourth courtyard. Here, on the south side, look for the shrine of **Venugopala Krishnan**, with its charmingly sculpted figures in the famous Hoysala style of the temples at Belur and Halebid – notice the girl with the parakeet, who was important in Indian literature as the go-between bearing messages for passionate lovers.

Climb up to the terrace overlooking this shrine for an excellent **view** over the *gopurams* beyond the fourth courtyard to the golden *vimana*, the inner sanctum, and its arched roof with the god Vishnu portrayed on each side. Binoculars will be especially useful here.

That's not water in those pots, but potent fermented palm-toddy.

Most spectacular of all, though, set in the eastern courtyard of the fourth enclosure, is the **Sesharyar** worship-hall with its eight carved pillars of rearing horses and their proud warriors. The energy of these minutely detailed sculptures from the 16th century, which honour the military prowess of the then great Vijayanagar kingdom, is a climax of south Indian art.

Thanjavur

Known to the British as Tanjore, this was the historic capital of the great Chola kingdom which spread Tamil culture to Burma, China and South-east Asia, where its artful sculpture and architecture can be seen to this day in the temples of Cambodia, Thailand and Java.

Commercial enterprise, military power and religious fervour went together. More than the divinity of Shiva, the 11th-century **Temple of Brihadisvara** boasts architecture celebrating the victory of the great Chola kingdom over the Pallavas of Kanchipuram and the Cheras of Kerala.

The accent is on the grandiose: the temple's main *vimana* shrine consisting of a massive, 13-tiered pyramid some 66 m (222 ft) high.

Shiva's sacred bull, Nandi, is built on a similarly colossal scale, as is the phallic lingam, which is believed to be the biggest in India. Frescoes depict in gory detail that head-chopping was necessary to achieve victory. However, a much more graceful architectural touch can be seen in the panels of Shiva demonstrating the 108 basic poses performed in the sacred dance – *bharata natyam* (see p. 199).

Ivy League Connection
Among the memorials to British heroes in St. Mary's, Americans may be pleased to see a plaque honouring the subsequent founder of one of its great universities, Elihu Yale, a former governor of the Fort. But Yaley has nothing to be proud of here. The merchant was fired in 1692 after five years as governor for making a large and dubious fortune while being in the service of the East India Company. New England clergy-man Cotton Mather, himself a Harvard man, got Yale to part with some of his ill-gotten gains to endow a new college to be named after him if he was the biggest donor. Elihu sent a parcel of goods that sold for £562, but no-body did better.

MADRAS

Madras is easy-going and pleasant, and it's remarkably uncrowded.

The beach for relaxing here is an amazing 12 km (7 miles) long, but Madras is also *the* place for banking and mailing packages, and for picking up letters from home at the *poste restante* counter of the General Post Office.

Madras was set up in 1642 as the East India Company's first east coast trading station, for shipping cotton and sugar. After the defeat of the French, it took a grateful

Madras's memory of its Victorian age is more serene than that of other big Indian towns.

back seat in Indian affairs, far away from the turmoils of northern India. These days, fiercely independent-minded Tamil politics make the place much more lively and alert at election time, but less heated than, say, the cities of Calcutta, Bombay or the Punjab.

Doubting Thomas

When Jesus was arranging the disciples' assignments to spread the Good Word around the world, the disciple Thomas was given India to cover.

'Whithersoever thou wilt, Lord, send me,' said Thomas, as it is written in the Apocryphal Acts of the Apostles, 'but to India, I will not go.'

Then Gondophernes, a Pahlava king on the north-west frontier, sent for a master carpenter to help with the building of a new city. Thomas's professional pride overcame his hesitant evangelistic fervour and he realized it was an offer he couldn't refuse.

He converted Gondophernes and proselytized throughout the south to the Coromandel coast, where he is said to have suffered martyrdom, and was speared to death while praying in a cave in the south-west corner of modern Madras.

Fort St. George is the home of Tamil Nadu's State government and the Indian Navy. There is a **Military Museum**, and a British 'relic' inside the Fort: **St. Mary's Church**, in the style of Wren.

The most picturesque street in the old town, across the railway tracks north of the Fort (an area once known as 'Black Town') is **Armenian Street.** Still the centre of a small Armenian community, there's a busy street-market and, in a cool, tree-shaded garden, an open-air colonnaded church.

The **State Museum** situated on Pantheon Road possesses excellent Buddhist bronzes and a detailed collection of Dravidian sculpture and architecture. From 9th-century Pallavas and Cholas to the rich style of the Vijayanagar kingdom (1336-1565), the exhibits make a fascinating demonstration in stone of the glory of south India.

The two main arteries of the city are the busy shopping centre along Mount Road, and Beach Avenue, where you'll find the University, Madras Cricket Club and **San Thomé Cathedral.** This simple, even austere, neo-Gothic Catholic church houses what is claimed to be the tomb of St. Thomas.

Mahabalipuram

The ancient port of the Pallava kings, a high point in any tour of south Indian monuments, is only 60 km (36 miles) south of Madras, but you are strongly recommended to stay there overnight if possible, rather than making a day-trip from Madras. It has accommodation on the beach, enabling you to see the cliff-carvings, *ratha* shrines and Shore Temple by the sea in the early morning and at night.

Originally the town was known as Mamallapuram, being named after King Narasimha Mamalla (630–668), 'the great wrestler', in whose reign its many extraordinary temples and shrines were begun.

Like the cave-temples of Ellora (see p. 118), most monuments are carved, rather than built, from solid rock, in this case the last cliffs and boulders of the vast granite plateau that ends at the Coromandel coast.

South of the village is a set of **Rathas**, monolithic shrines hewn from one table of rock. Imitating elements of the region's wooden and brick-construction, some have the same arched and domed roofs as the inner *vimana* sanctuaries which you can see at Srirangam and at Thanjavur (see p. 186).

The largest shrine, the three-storeyed pyramidal **Dharmaraja**, at the southern end has 50 figures including its gods and heroes, and fascinatingly, modest subjects such as temple-servants.

Of the rock-carvings north of the *rathas*, the most celebrated is **The Great Penance.** The narrative sculpture panels cover an entire cliff-face, in which a natural split in the rock has been assimilated as the Ganga river as it descends through the hair of Shiva.

The **Shore Temple**, which has withstood the wind and the waves for 12 centuries is made up of two shrines. Shiva the Destroyer faces dangers at sea while Vishnu the Preserver watches over the town.

The temple is clearly inspired by the styling of the monolithic Dharmaraja shrine, but it is more tapered because originally it had to double as a lighthouse with a bright beacon burning at the apex.

Kanchipuram

Kanchi, 'Golden City, has scores of temples, hundreds if you include the shrines, dedicated to Vishnu and Shiva, and it is highly revered as one of the seven holy cities of ancient India – the others are:

Varanasi, Mathura, Hardwar and Dwarka and Ayodhya.

It's an easy trip to make from Mahabalipuram and you can shop in Kanchipuram for silk.

Kailasanatha is one of the most important Shiva sanctuaries dating from the 8th century. The sandstone temple on a granite base has some graceful sculptures court of Shiva and Parvati as a celestial king and queen receiving homage from their subjects, at their home on Mount Kailasa.

Vaikuntaperumal is a Vishnu temple of the same period, famous for its elevated colonnade of lively sculpted reliefs showing the many exploits of the Pallava kings.

Pondicherry

The most visible Gallic touch in this bastion of the French colonial adventure in India is the scarlet *képi* worn by the white-uniformed traffic police waving you on as you drive into town.

Many of the street-names are still French – Rue Suffren, Rue Lauriston, Rue Dumas (Alexandre) and Rue Dupleix, today known as Rue Jawaharlal Nehru. However, only few people speak French here today. The French War Memorial

Kanchipuram is equally proud of its temples and superlative silk.

on the coast road stands opposite a monument to Gandhi.

After 250 years of French rule in Pondicherry, the Indians were fortunate to have the decolonizer, Pierre Mendès-France, to deal with when it was retrieved in 1954.

Apart from the pleasant white sandy **beach**, for nostalgics of the 1960s there's a pilgrimage to be made to the inspirational 'Mecca' – **Auroville.** This spiritual retreat was started in 1968 by a French disciple of the self-help teachings of the Indian sage, Sri Aurobindo. It has lost some of its dynamism with the squabbles following the death of the founder, The Mother.

But the 'organic' forms of the buildings, with names like Hope, Fraternity and Aspiration, 10 km (6 miles) north of Pondicherry, still have an impact on the landscape. As Scandinavians and Bavarians cycle by, 1968 seems as remote as when the first cattle-herders came here from the other side of India, 3,500 years ago. The Dravidians were already there to meet them.

191

WHAT TO DO

Sports

What the Indians enjoyed about the British was their enthusiasm for sport, which included hockey and cricket in particular. In return, the British learned the delights of polo – imported with the Mughals from Persia and Afghanistan – and a kind of game-hunting that made grouse-shooting seem tame.

Today, with the exception of game-hunting, sporting life in India is still very active. Just be careful to adapt yourself to the climate, and avoid going out in the midday sun.

Delhi has very modern facilities since the Asian Games in 1982.

Participant Sports
Swimming is a natural first choice. Many first-class hotels in leading cities have swimming pools, but there are a precautions you should take when swimming elsewhere.

After all that sightseeing, cool off on a Goa beach.

For health reasons it is best to avoid swimming in rivers, ponds, lakes and reservoirs – your body is unlikely to be able to deal with some of the other things swimming around with you.

Beach swimming is best at the recognized resorts rather than the major port-cities. In Bombay, both Juhu and Chowpatty beaches are, for instance, definitely not a good idea, and though the Marina beaches in Madras are cleaner, there may even be sharks.

The best resort beaches are on the Malabar coast at Kovalam, Goa and, smaller but charming, Cochin. Kovalam also has **surfing,** but be careful as there are strong currents. On the east coast, try Puri, south of Calcutta, or Pondicherry.

Sailing is possible at most of the resorts. In Madras, you can rent a catamaran and, if you're staying at the Taj in Bombay, you should be able to get a guest-membership at the nearby Yacht Club.

Fishing is very popular in India and although it is almost entirely a freshwater proposition, you will find it very good. The indigenous mahseer, a distant relative of the carp, and which can weigh as much as 20 kg (44 lb), is considered by

193

many sportsmen to be as good a sporting challenge as the salmon.

The best fishing is in Kashmir. The streams were long ago stocked with brown trout from Scotland.

Cricket is more than a sport in India, it's an obsession.

You will find more information and a fishing permit available at the Directory of Fisheries in the tourist office building based in Srinagar. The tourist office in Delhi can give information and permits for fishing in the Yamuna river and, similarly, the tourist office in Bangalore for fishing in the Cauvery river.

Hiking or **trekking,** as it is most often called here, is a marvellous way of getting away from the often madding crowd in India and you will find it is well organized in the old hill stations.

Travel agencies happily provide a range of camping and cooking equipment, as well as the guides, cooks and porters you need, and a jeep for travelling to more remote and inaccessible areas.

Once again, Kashmir is a choice region, but try Simla, Darjeeling, Sikkim and, much closer to Delhi, the Naini Tal region. The necessary arrangements for this can easily be improvised on the spot, but a more ambitious six – or seven-day trek needs some notice, so it would be best to book this with your travel agent and settle the details before you leave home.

Golf and **tennis** fans will find these activities are available in the major cities. Golfers should apply for a guest-membership from the many clubs the Indians inherited from the British. Tennis lovers will find there are courts in the major hotels or in public parks.

Many of these hotels also have a health-club with a **gym** or **yoga** class, the real thing.

Spectator Sports

The most beloved sport in India by far, is **cricket**. There's something in the intricacy of its arcane rules and controlled passion that appeals to the Indian people.

It's an astounding obsession – and all major cities have stadiums. The most fervent atmosphere of all is at the Calcutta Cricket Club, founded in 1792, five years after the Marylebone Cricket Club in London. The Brabourne Stadium in Bombay is more relaxed. If you don't catch a major match, you're may come across one in an alley of Calcutta or a meadow in Kashmir.

Hockey is a British import, in which the Indians have surpassed their former masters. Today they often share the Olympic finals with their old arch-rivals, Pakistan.

Polo is a Rajasthan speciality, but tournaments are also held in Delhi and Bombay in the winter months. It is a rich man's sport.

Horse-racing is popular with races such as the Calcutta Derby, St. Leger and the Oaks in Bombay. The highest course in the country is at Darjeeling. **Camel-racing** is also big at Jaisalmer in February and also at the autumn festival at Pushkar (see p. 202).

Entertainment

One of the many pleasant surprises in India is the way that its classical **music** – heard perhaps in snatches back in the West and dismissed as something hopelessly beyond an ordinary Westerner's appreciation – grows on you when you hear it in the country of its creation.

In order to make things easier, rather than what might have been the intimidating atmosphere of a large recital-hall, a first encounter with Indian music is most likely to be in the pleasant surroundings of a restaurant in one of the smarter hotels, where it may be performed as the accompaniment to an elegant dinner, with first-class musicians.

In its own way, it takes its hold on you – alternately soothing and lulling, fascinating – and before you know it, you're hooked.

The music consists of two basic elements: the *raga*, the melody of five or more notes, and the *tala*, the rhythm or tempo. Improvisation is of the essence. In a prelude or *alap,* which in full-length recitals can last half an hour, the lead musician seems to grope around until the main theme and its many variations take hold and patterns emerge from the apparent confusion.

Like the musicians themselves, give yourself up to the hypnotic effect of the notes, rhythms and melodies or even silences. A fully realized performance could go on for two or three hours (shorter in restaurant recitals). It is perfectly normal at a concert for people to walk around, fidget and talk at the beginning of the recital until the music asserts itself.

Apart from the music played in the big cities and the sophisticated music of the Brahmanic tradition, you can listen to the folk-music of Rajasthan, rousing or plaintive, in one of those abandoned villages in the desert around Jaisalmer.

Song, using rhythm and melody in the same way as instrumental music, is religious and romantic in content. South Indian song is both joyful and sad. In the north, where song was subject to Arabian and Persian influences, it varies from *dhrupad*, meaning austere, without embellishment, and the more florid *khyal*, India's version of *bel canto*, or *thumri*, the style of light-hearted, tender love songs.

Kathakali *dancers in the South take hours to put on that make-up.*

Sitar and Company

Indian music is played not by a full orchestra, but usually by two or three instrumentalists, all sitting cross-legged. One of the principal instruments, made famous in the West by Ravi Shankar, is the long six-stringed sitar *with its bulbous sound-box. The robust* sarangi *is played with a bow, joined in the past couple of centuries by the Western violin, but played vertically, with its base held by the musician's bare right foot. The accompanist's four-stringed* tambura *provides the music's resonant ambience.*

The ancient vina, *a seven-stringed lute with a rounded body at the base and highly coloured bowl at the top, was played by the goddess Sarasvati, muse of the arts, and just like the piano in the West, is played at home by respectable young ladies. The flute you'll see is essentially the same as the one used by Krishna.*

There are two kinds of percussion: the small twin drums of the Indian tabla *and the long bulging* mridangam *drum of south India, which is held horizontally with the right hand providing a high-pitched tone for the melody and the left hand beating a deeper tone for the rhythm.*

In addition to this dinner music, the major hotels organize full-scale recitals of music, song and dance, and so if you do acquire a taste for it, look out for concerts in town – Delhi has recitals around Republic Day at the end of January.

Indian **dance** is marvellously expressive, with every gesture and movement signifying a vocabulary of emotions. Like the sculptures on the temples, the eloquence of dance was a means of transmitting the messages of the holy scriptures and adventures of the great Hindu epics to its listeners.

Classical sacred dance, *bharata natyam*, has a total of 108 different consecrated forms – and you can see them performed by Shiva, in the sculpted frieze of Thanjavur's Brihadisvara Temple (see p. 186). Originally, these holy dances were performed by *devadasis*, the sacred dancing-girls, who were in fact the temple prostitutes – that is until the Hindu reform movement during the 19th century made it acceptable for girls of respectable families to perform the dances, too.

In Kerala, try to see the lively *kathakali* dances, in which men play both male and female parts to enact both divine and heroic Indian legends in the most gorgeous costumes and elaborate make-up. Performances of musical works are regularly held in Cochin's neighbouring town of Ernakulam. The more sophisticated dance found in eastern India is known as *odissi*.

Film in India, produced mainly in the cities of Madras, Bombay, Calcutta and Bangalore, is a major industry, if only rarely an art, and the large scale production of entertainment films is a phenomenon well worth seeing seveeal times. You may well be more baffled by the appeal of the colourful musical comedies and violent shoot-emups than you would be in the West, but the emotion of the melodramas and romantic adventure stories of India's cultural and historic past have considerable curiosity value for a rainy afternoon. If you watch the action closely, you can learn a lot about Indian people by what makes them cheer, laugh or weep.

Calcutta seems to be the only other production-centre having any pretensions to artistic creativity at all, but ironically you're actually more likely to see the works of Satyajit Ray or Mrinal Sen shown in Europe or North America than in India itself.

199

Festivals and Fairs

You could probably spend your whole time in India going to festivals. In a country with such a strong and varied religious tradition and a vital need to have a good time, there's always some reason for celebrating something with a parade. The festivals and fairs bring together a mixture of fakirs and fortune-tellers, snake-dancers and charlatans. Want to buy a used camel?

Here are a selection (the dates are uncertain because they follow a lunar calendar):

January: *Pongal*, in Trichy and Madurai; a three-day harvest festival during which cows and bullocks are fed with harvested rice. The atmosphere is generally jolly, but the highlight is a variation on the universal bullfight in which young men try to pluck rupee notes that have been spiked on the horns of a very angry bull.

January 26: *Republic Day*, Delhi; great march-past in which India shows off its cultural diversity and military might, the latter softened by a helicopter flying overhead disguised as a flying elephant with the pilot dropping rose-petals on the crowd.

January/February: *Vasant Panchami*, throughout India but best seen in Calcutta; honouring Sarasvati, goddess of scholars and artists. Everyone dresses up in bright yellow and flies kites.

January/February: *Desert Festival*, Jaisalmer; a lively celebration of Rajasthani music and dance, plus camel-races in the local stadium.

February/March: *Mardi Gras*, Goa; the Catholic carnival, with a hint of Portugal mixed with a sweet-smelling whiff of India. Costumes and masks and dancing in the streets.

February/March: *Shivratri*, Khajuraho and Varanasi; solemn celebration of Shiva, with all-night music and prayers in the temples.

February/March: *Holi*, northern India, best at Mathura, south of Delhi; the spring festival when lovers (and others) spray each other with coloured powder and water.

March/April: *Gangaur*, Udaipur and Jaipur; very colourful procession of girls balancing on their head four or five brilliantly polished brass pitchers with which they bathe Shiva's wife Parvati (Gauri). The garlanded deity is then accompanied by Shiva at the head of a parade of horses and elephants.

April/May: *Spring Festival*, Srinagar; Kashmiris bring out their samovars for a big tea party to celebrate the first pink and white almond blossoms, highlighted by mid-April festivities in the Mughal Gardens.

At the Puri Rath Yatra *festival, fanatics have been known to crush themselves to death beneath a wheel of Jaggannath's temple-chariot.*

April/May: *Baisakhi*, all over north India; the Hindus' solar New Year. The Sikhs celebrate the anniversary of Guru Gobind Singh's exhortation to form the *khalsa* ('army of the pure').

July: *Rath Yatra*, Puri; one of the greatest festivals of the year, when the three gigantic temple-chariots of Jaggannath, his brother Balabhadra and sister Subhadra are drawn through the streets (see p. 154).

July/August: *Amarnath Yatra*, Kashmir; during the full moon, thousands of pilgrims make their way from Pahalgam to the cave of Amarnath to Shiva's ice-stalagmite lingam.

September/October: *Dussehra*, Mysore, Delhi and Calcutta; ten days of pageant and pomp in elephant processions following behind the Maharaja of Mysore's throne. In north India, there are music, dance and drama centring in Delhi on the legendary hero Rama (with fireworks blowing up his demon enemy Ravana), and in Calcutta, on the goddess Durga.

October/November: *Pushkar Fair*; this is Rajasthan's big show – camels, horses and bullocks are brought from everywhere to be sold at the market. The camel races are spectacular and this is a fine place to buy Rajasthani craftwork, especially bangles and necklaces.

October/November: *Divali*, all over India; the happiest of festivals, a combination of Mardi Gras and Christmas, honouring Lakshmi, goddess of prosperity, except in Bengal, where they honour their goddess Kali, no less merrily, immersing her in the Hooghly river.

November: *Sonepur Cattle Fair*, near Patna; on the banks of the Ganga, this month-long cattle and elephant market is one of the world's biggest, bringing all the usual colourful eccentrics into town.

December 25: *Christmas*, Bombay and Goa; a more religious observance than in most Western countries.

Variable dates:

Muharram, Lucknow; Moslem mourning for Imam Hussein, grandson of Mohammed, when spectacular illuminated bamboo and paper replicas of the martyr's tomb are paraded through the town.

Id-ul-Fitr, Lucknow, Delhi and Calcutta; mosques are lit up as Moslems celebrate the end of the Ramadan fast.

Decorating a giant Divali *puppet in Goa has all the high jinks of a Western Mardi Gras.*

Shopping

From the Greeks to the Turks and Mughals, from Marco Polo to Lord Mountbatten, all were seduced by India's riches, and it's still a great place to shop.

As in any ancient country, its modernizing plunge into the 20th century has produced its fair share of junk and tawdry tinsel, but its traditional craftwork continues at the highest level: silks and carpets, jewellery, perfumes, brassware and wood-carving are first class, and you will have the added bonus of dealing with the most charming bunch of merchants in the world – the scoundrels, that is *particularly* the scoundrels.

At least half the pleasure is in the bargaining. If you don't want to be fleeced, don't plunge in blindly. Go first to the Government Cottage Industry Emporiums, which can be found in almost every major city. The selection here is not usually as wide as you'll find in the privately run shops and you can't haggle, but it'll give you an idea of the range of goods, quality and, above all, the reasonable price.

Then you're ready for the fray, either in the bustling great bazaars such as Delhi's Chandni Chowk

Feeling the merchandise before the lively haggling starts in this Calangute beach-bazaar.

or Bombay's Bhuleshwar, or the more sedate ambience of grander shops and showrooms. The one street-market you shouldn't miss is Bombay's Chor Bazaar or Thieves' Market, which is an extravagant flea market where, among other things, you'll see Indian motorists buying back spare parts stolen from their cars the night before.

If, during your tours of the big cities, you come across products you like from places you will be visiting later, such as Rajasthan, Varanasi or Kashmir, wait until you get there – the price and selection may be much better.

meet some down in the plains, to which, like many other wily birds, they migrate in the winter.

If there's no magic formula for the perfect bargain – each person will have his own psychological approach – you should avoid two extremes: don't be too eager, and don't, on the other hand, assume everybody is out to cheat you. It spoils the sport.

Carpets, then, are one of the most attractive purchases you can make. Ever since the days when the Mughal emperor Jahangir took Persian craftsmen up to Kashmir with him during his long summer holidays, the handwoven silk and woollen carpets of Srinagar have been among the best in the world.

The silk gives the carpets their unique sheen. The prices will vary according to the proportions of silk and wool used and the density of the weave itself, and naturally none of them are cheap.

Look out for traditional Persian and original Kashmiri motifs such as peacocks and fruit trees, tiger-hunts and Mughal lovers. Indeed many of the carpets seem just too lovely to walk on, but they make superb wall-hangings, and even if you can't remortgage your house

Haggling with dapper Gujaratis and the bright-eyed Kashmiris can attain the level of high art. Even if you don't land a bargain, there is real aesthetic pleasure, in seeing at the end of the verbal 'combat', the disarray of silks thrown across a counter or a mound of carpets on the floor. The Kashmiris' wizardry is at its best on the floating market of their *shikaras*, but you can also

to buy a big one, even a modest bedside rug can simply do wonders to warm and brighten your room on a cold winter morning.

Cashmere is the one thing the Kashmiris are touchy about. That '100% cashmere' label you show them on your best sweater could provoke a loud snort of 'Scotland!' or even 'Australia!', but then, like an endearment to a beloved one, they will murmur '*pashmina*' and spread before you a shawl of soft,

Mother knows just what she wants, but her demure daughter hesitates.

warm wool shorn, they tell you, from the underbelly of the wild Himalayan goats. Then, just when you think you've never touched anything finer, they turn around and whisper 'shahtoosh', the finest Kashmir wool of all, taken from the throat of the ibex and woven so finely that they can pass a shawl right through a wedding-ring.

These, too, are expensive, but you can get shawls of good quality wool with distinctive embroidery, and at more reasonable prices.

Silks have long been basic to a fine Indian lady's wardrobe and make magnificent tunics, blouses, stoles or long, trailing scarves for a Western outfit.

The question may arises as to whether Western women can wear a *sari* or other traditional Indian costumes. It is, of course, a matter of personal taste, of how 'Indian' a woman will feel or *look*, since blondes often seem incongruous in a sari. The costume most easily adapted to Western tastes, perhaps because it involves trousers, seems to be a long tunic worn over baggy pantaloons with a soft stole around the shoulders, known as *salwar kameez*, most popular in the north-west, and very elegant.

Three towns hare famous for their silk: Bangalore, for its classic printed silk; Varanasi, for its gold and silver brocades; Kanchipuram, for its heavy, brilliantly coloured silk, favoured for formal saris and, not forgetting the men, the city of Kanchipuram also produces superb silk ties.

Cottons, either handprinted or embroidered, are probably the best bargain of all India's textiles: table-cloths, napkins, bed-linen – not to mention spreads and pillow-cases – as well as airy light scarves that make life much more comfortable in the Indian heat. Indian tailors are cheap, good and fast, so you might consider having lightweight shirts and baggy pants made up specially for you during your stay.

Three cotton-prints to look out for, particularly in Rajasthan, are: *bagru*, consisting of geometric or fish, almond and vine patterns in blue, brown and maroon colours; *sanganeri*, block printed floral and paisley patterns; and *bandhani*, tie-dye, which gives decorative colour. The bright motifs with mirror-glass stitched into them, much favoured by Rajasthani ladies of the desert for their long flowing skirts, are known as *cutchhi* or *saurashtra*.

207

SHOPPING

The dashing, rather coarse cotton Punjabi *phulkari* shawls are made from fabric with patterns in orange, pink, green, red and yellow.

Jewellery is important here – precious and semi-precious stones. The jewellery of Rajasthan is much sought after.

Indian diamond mines produced some of the world's greatest gems, including the Kohi-nur (Mountain of Light), now in the British crown jewels, having originally been in the Peacock Throne. Although the mines are superseded by those in South America and South Africa, the art of cutting and polishing has remained in Gujarat. Bombay is a centre for importing rough-cuts and selling 'finished product'.

Don't buy any unless you are or have an expert with you. Diamonds are graded from D to X, with only D, E, and F considered as good, D being colourless or 'river white', J 'slightly tinted', Q 'light yellow' and S to X 'yellow'.

The essential piece of jewellery in India however, is the bangle. Whole stalls are devoted to it, made from silver and gold, metal, wood, glass, plastic, and – best bargain of all – colourful varnished papier-mâché from Kashmir.

Gold, silver, copper and brass – each has its own bazaar in the big neighbourhood markets of Delhi, Bombay and Calcutta. Of these, the most well-known is Jains' Zaveri Bazaar in Bombay, where antique gold is sold.

The wood carvings vary from rosewood elephants or sandalwood camels to the Kashmiris' finely fretted walnut work, created in the style of the screens on the Srinagar houseboats.

For more modern painting, try the art galleries around Connaught Place in New Delhi, and Bombay's Pundole and Chemould Galleries, not to forget the Academy of Fine Arts in Calcutta.

Cooks will be on the look-out for spices, which we recommend you not to buy until your last day: chilli, turmeric, cardamom, ginger nutmeg and cumin. The best places to buy Indian spices, however, are the Khadi Bhandars, because they are government supervised, so the spices are not adulterated.

Tea gourmets will make a bee-line for Darjeeling, where you can buy directly from the plantations or at the town bazaar. When you buy a couple of kilos, they'll ship it for you in air-tight packages.

EATING OUT

India's fine cuisine is as rich and
diverse as its civilization and, since
Indians don't go out to restaurants,
home-cooking is best. Major hotels
and first-class restaurants will give
you the opportunity to taste various
regional dishes.

The dishes are highly seasoned,
but the spices are subtle and it will
take some time for you to get used
to it, even if you're familiar with
Indian cuisine back home.

Although hotels are at pains not
to overdo the hotter spices, it's still
likely to be much sharper than you
will be used to. So, take it easy – a
little at a time.

You should not expect each day
to be a major culinary adventure.
Even if your tastes are very simple,
you may be quickly bored by the
food in the more modest establishments and smaller towns.

On the other hand, it would be
silly to steer away completely from
local food. It's unlikely that you
came to India to eat the same food
that you're used to back home. In
any case, Indians are much better at
cooking Indian food than what the
menu calls 'Continental', i.e. bland
all-purpose Western meals. Few

209

hotels break the beef taboo to serve steaks or hamburgers, though even they may be buffalo meat. If you plump for a mediocre Western meal occasionally, the best is to 'go Chinese', something the Indians do much better than 'Continental'.

Breakfast

All the trimmings of British breakfasts are usually available: porridge (oatmeal), cereals, eggs and bacon, with tropical fresh seasonal fruits such as mango, papayas and pineapples, and their juices.

Coffee in north India is usually instant, but do ask for the excellent Madras brew wherever it's available. Tea is rarely Darjeeling, but yoiu'll find the Assam type is as good as any in British hotels. For safety's sake the milk is boiled, and re-cooled for the cereals.

Indian-style breakfasts may be rice and curried vegetables, with a drink of *lassi*, cold liquid yoghurt, which is either sweet or seasoned with salt or cumin. In the south, you'll find *idli, dosa and hoppers*– different forms of rice and lentil – flour pancakes – which may be folded around mixed, mildly spicy vegetables like an omelette, and served with fruit chutneys.

Lunch and Dinner

If you have plenty of things to do in the afternoon, keep lunch light and plan your gastronomic adventure for around 8 pm to give yourself plenty of time to digest it.

Try scooping up your own spicy mixture – it is a delicate art.

Hotels will often provide large buffets, giving you a chance to try several dishes, which people tend to pile up on one plate around a large mound of rice, but traditional Indian meals are served on a *thali*, a large metal platter, with each dish in a separate little bowl, *katori*, so that you can savour the different tastes separately.

Places that have assimilated the British custom will serve a soup like *mulligatawny* – which is a spicy chicken, mutton or vegetable broth created for colonial officials. Otherwise, with the exception of the food served at great banquets, meals are not divided into courses, everything will usually arrive on your *thali* at the same time.

You'll find it good to follow the Indian custom of drinking something either before or after, but not during a meal. Drinking does not in the end alleviate a peppery flavour because it will leave your tastebuds completely defenceless against the next hot mouthful. Therefore, it's better to eat some plain rice, or one of the soft Indian breads, or fruit, or best of all, yoghurt.

The utensils and primus stove are modern, but the chapati *recipe is as old as India.*

Indians eat with their fingers, rotating the finger tips around the plate to form the food into a ball with rice or bread. Cutlery may be provided, but a fork may not be any more hygienic than fingers.

212

'Curry'

Properly speaking, there's no such thing. It's a British term invented to refer indiscriminately to India's spicy preparations of fish, meat and vegetables. It has been traced to the Tamil word *kari*, meaning quite simply 'sauce'.

In India there is not one 'curry powder' or 'curry sauce', because each dish has its own combination of spices.

The combination of spices used is known as *masala*, the mixing of hot chilli, coriander, cumin, ginger and turmeric together with garlic and onions. The other mixture is *garam masala*, a blend of cloves, cinnamon, cardamom, nutmeg and mace. Saffron adds its own unique colour and fragrance, both to rice and to meat. In fine establishments, it's even used to perfume the room before the meal begins.

Non-Vegetarian

The classical cuisine of the north, *mughlai*, comes from the Mughals.

With beef taboo for Hindus and pork for Moslems, the meat is lamb or mutton, its classic 'curry' being *rogan josh*. The cubes of meat are prepared in a yoghurt sauce made with chilli, ginger, coriander and turmeric and *garam masala*. This dish originated in Kashmir, where they eat lamb in dozens of different ways (if you attend a *wazwan* banquet, there may be as many as 16, 36 or even 52 dishes.).

Other dishes are the *kebab*, balls of lamb minced with almonds and spices; *tabakmas*, mutton ribs with a crispy skin; and *goshtaba*, the tenderest lamb from the breast, with every last sinew beaten out of it before it is minced into a fragrant

---

The Spice of Life

You may be pleased to know that, according to the ancient canons of Indian medicine, the myriad spices concealed in your meal are all working to improve your health. While the combination stimulates the appetite and helps your digestion in this very special climate, some of the individual spices have surprising properties.

Turmeric is very good for skin ailments, ginger for your liver or rheumatism. Cloves can help the kidneys, relieve fever and also stimulate the heart. Coriander fights constipation and insomnia, but one of the most versatile is cardamom, battling bad breath, headaches, throaty coughs, and haemorrhoids.

> ### Goa For Gourmets
> *The old Portuguese colony, with a large Christian community, holds a unique position on the country's gastronomic map. Happy to use pork and beef in its very spicy 'curries' and pungent sausages, it also makes splendid use of the abundant seafood available on its Malabar coast.*
>
> *Tisryo is a delicate dish of tiny stewed clams, spiced with ginger and sprinkled with coconut. But its most celebrated dish, simply consecrated as* Goanese *curry, is oriental bouillabaisse, a thick sauce of tamarind and coconut, onions and tomatoes served over diverse local fish such as clams, shrimps, crabs and any other types the fishermen have caught that day, all of it spiced to the gills. It's the Sunday lunch, but it's usually enough for a whole week. You probably won't have room for an* alebele, *a sweet and spicy crêpe which is stuffed with coconut. Save that one for Monday, with the potent* feni, *a fermented cashew drink.*

dumpling stewed in yoghurt. In Kashmir it is the climactic dish of a wedding banquet – after eating the liver, the kidneys, the shoulder, the leg, and various minced kebabs.

Biriani is a Mughlai speciality originally exclusively a lamb dish, though chicken, fish and vegetables are now cooked in the same way.

This dish is more elaborate than *pulao*, which is a simple mixture of rice and lightly flavoured meat or vegetablse. *Biriani* is chicken or lamb cooked in a sauce of ginger, cardamom, cinammon and cloves before steaming it with saffron rice and *ghee* (clarified butter). It may be served decorated with almonds and mint – and with a thin film of edible silver, adding luxury to the dish, but not the taste.

Chickens tend to be scrawny, but they are tasty in a *makhni* butter sauce as *murg ilaychi*, marinated in yoghurt with cardamom, ginger, peppers and saffron, or *murg do pyaza*, with shallots and onions.

Tandoori chicken is a popular barbecue in north-west style baked in a *tandoor* clay oven. Typically, the chicken is salted and doused in lime juice, tenderized with papaya, then marinated in yoghurt with a flavouring of ginger, garlic, chilli and saffron, before being plunged on a spit into the charcoal-heated oven. Fish and giant prawns, marinated in different sauces, also make very good *tandoori* dishes.

Rice and Chapatis

The best rice is the aromatic long-grained *basmati*, the common or garden variety known as *patna*.

Apart from *biriani* and *pulao*, the north Indian cuisine does not feature the large quantities of rice of south Indian cuisine The Indians in the north prefer to eat their food with a variety of breads, including a floppy, thin *roti* or *chapati*, and a slightly thicker *paratha*, sometimes stuffed with vegetables or minced meat, small deep-fried *puri* or giant puffed up *nan*, baked in a *tandoor*. Here is a tip: before you tackle the rice dishes of the south, try eating with your fingers in the north, by folding a piece of *roti* around each morsel.

Vegetarian

Favourite vegetable dishes are *aloo gobi* (cauliflower and potato) and *bharta* (curried eggplant), as well as *sag panir* (spinach with cottage-cheese). You could also try *sabzi bhindi* (lady's fingers with cumin, peppers and onions). These dishes are served with chickpeas or a *thali* platter, or a bowl of *dal* – a subtly spiced porridge of lentils, which come round or flat, and which are mostly yellow or red.

In addition to the fresh seafood cooked and eaten particularly in the kitchens of Goa, the cuisine of southern India is more vegetarian than in the north. This is for the economic reason of not having the meat available, but also because the region was not subject to the Mughal influence.

Whereas the north cooks with the products of its cattle, such as *ghee* for frying, yoghurt for sauces and milk for desserts, the basis of southern cooking is the *coconut* – its oil is used for frying, and the milk and flesh for sauces. This does give the food a sweeter taste than in other regions. Sauces, in which water, vinegar or coconut milk is added to the spices, are more liquid, gradually absorbed by the rice as the meal progresses.

> **Very Fishy**
> The strictest vegetarians exclude fish, meat, poultry and eggs, even blood-coloured vegetables such as beetroot or tomato, quoting the ancient Sanskrit verse: 'In the next world animals will eat those who eat them in this world.' Some Brahmans of Bengal get around their partiality to fish by calling them 'fruit of the sea'.

The trouble with those delicious buffets is knowing when to stop.

Side-dishes and Snacks

Salads don't exist in the Western sense, but *cachumbar* is a refreshing side-dish of tomato and onion seasoned with fresh lemon juice or vinegar. The great palate-cooler, eaten both in the north and south, is *raita*, a mixture of cold yoghurt seasoned with cucumber, tomato or even pineapple.

As a sweet condiment, Indians serve not only mango, but mint and coconut, fresh ginger, tomato, dates or even tamarind as a spicy chutney (or more properly *chatni*). You'll find some of the flavours in these dishes pack an astonishing double punch of sweet and sharp.

There are some tangy Indian snacks to eat. Bombay's best is the *bhelpuri* sold on Chowpatty Beach (see p. 128), a pasty stuffed with fried chickpeas, noodles, herbs and chutney. S*amosas* are stuffed with meat or vegetables and *pakora* is a vegetable fritter. *Pani puri* is a pasty stuffed with tamarind water so you should put the whole thing in your mouth at once.

Desserts

Ras malai are patties made from cottage cheese and nuts, sweetened with aromatic syrup and perfumed with rose water and cardamom.

Khir is rice pudding. Yes, folks, it was invented here – made with condensed milk and broken rice, but much superior with cardamom and nuts. *Gajar halwa*, a dessert of grated carrots stewed in milk and syrup, is best hot, with raisins and nuts. *Kulfi* is ice-cream made with cardamom and pistachio. *Barfi* and *halwa* are sweets made with flour or milk and flavoured with nuts and fresh cardamom.

Drinks

The most cooling drinks are *nimbu pani* (fresh lime) or the fruit juices, especially that which comes from the fragrant Kashmiri apple. Indian beers are acceptable, white wines drinkable and whisky tolerable.

European wines are exorbitant and frankly not a good thing to drink with curry anyway. Among traditional Indian alcoholic drinks are palm toddy in Kerala, rice beer in the Himalayan foothills, *asha*, and a meat-based (!) liqueur made in Rajasthan. In Goa people drink *feni* , a cashew-based liqueur.

BERLITZ-INFO

CONTENTS

A ACCOMMODATION

Indian tourist accommodation caters for all tastes. In big cities as well as in all major centres of tourist interest (such as Agra, Jaipur, Srinagar), there are luxury hotels. In former princely states, ancient maharajas' palaces have been converted into hotels; those in Rajasthan being very successful. Some have been taken over by large commercial groups, others are run by members of princely families. In most cases, however, their popularity has caused a rise in prices. In old 'British India', at cheaper rates, you can find the hotels of yore. Throughout the country there are numerous smaller but comfortable establishments at much lower rates.

If you are not travelling in an organized group or have no reservation, you should head straight for the local tourist office and consult the list of 'government approved' hotels, which guarantees minimum standards in terms of facilities and also of general hygiene.

If you land when tourist offices are closed, you will find that in almost every town, government-run **tourist bungalows, hotels,** or **lodges** provide satisfactory accommodation, where the rates vary according to the comfort sought, such as whether the rooms have air-conditioning and hot water.

Every locality also has a **rest-house** or **dak-bungalow,** which often constitute the best value for money in India, but you may need to bring your own bedding. Book these in advance from the administration's local head office (either the public works department or the local authorities), or you can simply turn up on the doorstep and be given a room. It is best not to chance your luck in tourist centres like Agra or Jaipur.

Most railway stations have **rest rooms** where you can stay for a night or a few hours. They are clean and cheap, and you must hold a valid railway ticket to qualify for one. Most establishments will ask you whether you want 'AC' rooms (Air-Conditioned) or 'non-AC'. From May to September it is wise to spend a few rupees more and enjoy a cool retreat.

Be wary of the water in the plastic flask near your bed. Water shortages and power cuts, frequent in summer, do not allow automatic discounts. In the cheaper hotels, check your bed-linen and do not hesitate to have it changed if necessary.

Officially, all foreigners are expected to pay their hotel bills in foreign exchange. This, however, is only really applicable to luxury establishments, since few others have access to the day's rate of exchange.

YMCA and **YWCA hostels** (couples, married or not, are accepted) are in every large town and provide adequate, often excellent, accommodation.

AIRPORTS

The international airports in Delhi and Bomba, welcome the bulk of tourists and visitors to India. Airports at Calcutta and Madras are also equipped to receive international flights.

Indira Gandhi International Airport, New Delhi, is located 20km (12 miles) south-west of the city. The terminal facilities include a buffet, a number of currency-exchange counters, as well as a luggage deposit facility, a hotel reservation, car-hire and pre-paid taxi counters, and a duty-free shop.

Bombay International Airport is situated 29km (18miles) north of the city centre. This is by far India's busiest airport, both for international and domestic services. Its international terminal (Sahar), which is based over 5km (3miles) away from the domestic terminal (Santa Cruz), but linked to it by a regular shuttle-bus service, has all the facilities of a modern airport. At peak hours, the journey from the centre to the airport can take one hour, so allow for transfer time.

Arrival (see also CUSTOMS, ENTRY AND EXIT REGULATIONS). On arrival you will be required to fill in a health card. These are generally distributed to passengers on board the plane. Visitors who do not have any dutiable goods or high value articles or foreign exchange in excess of US $1,000 or unaccompanied baggage, all of which have to be declared, can simply walk through the Green Channel. Others however, will have go to the Red Channel for the appropriate clearance.

Ground transport. Airport terminals are organised to provide you with a cheap bus ride into town at regular intervals, throughout the night if the airport is a busy one. Airport bus services can be found in smaller places. You are also assured of finding taxis and motor-rickshaws. Taxi-runs from the airport are based on set fares which will naturally vary from airport to airport. Convenient pre-paid taxi services operate in all the major cities. Elsewhere, a policeman at the gate will ask for your name and destination: but he isn't prying, he's simply curbing taxi-driver greed. You will also be given a complaint card with a telephone number you might want to keep handy. Taxi fares to destinations in town are generally posted up on signs near the airport taxi stand.

Departure. On leaving India, you will be required to pay an airport tax in rupees. Security checks at airports are particularly intensive.

ALCOHOL

Only one State in India, Mahatma Gandhi's home State of Gujarat, remains completely 'dry'. Alcohol is generally available elsewhere, except in very remote areas and in religious centres. The once compulsory All India Tourist Permit is no longer necessary. Some hotels will ask you to drink either in your room or in the hotel's licensed bar – but it's up to you to shake off the guilt complex. Other than luxury hotels, few restaurants are authorized to serve beer or other alcoholic drinks. The 1st and 7th of each month are dry days (no alcohol will be available anywhere) in Delhi, and the 1st and 10th in Bombay. The days vary from State to State.

C CIGARETTES, CIGARS AND TOBACCO

Tobacco products with Indian brand names are on sale everywhere. Some international companies manufacture their brands in India. Most people find Indian cigarettes acceptable. Indigenous pipe tobacco and cigars are not always easily available. If you are a compulsive smoker, try the *bidi*, a single leaf of tobacco rolled and filled with shredded tobacco.

The Sikh religion places a ban on smoking so you'll be asked to hand in all your tobacco at the entrance when visiting a *gurdwara* (Sikh temple).

CITY TRANSPORT

Taxis exist in all large cities. **Tourist cars** (chauffeur-driven) can be hired out in centres of tourist interest, through the local tourist office.

Other than airport-to-hotel journeys, which operate on a fixed fare, all drivers must use their meters. Meters, however, are generally out of date, and the driver will show a conversion chart for the fare.

Motor-rickshaws, also known as scooter-rickshaws (three-wheel mini-taxis) operate in a similar way. Again, fare rates vary from town to town; in general, a scooter-rickshaw fare is about half a normal taxi fare. Scooter-rickshaws are banned in Bombay's congested inner city zone, so there it has to be a taxi, bus or suburban train.

In all big cities, there is an efficient **bus** service which, when you know how to use the route guide available from all bookstalls, is convenient. The only problem is that buses in India carry large crowds.

There are also **cycle-rickshaws** and **tongas** (horse-drawn carts). You agree on the price before starting off. Calcutta and a few other places still have old-style **rickshaws,** pulled by men. Calcutta also has India's first **metro** (either subway or underground), line (crowded and hot, but cheap) and India's last operating **tram** service (less crowded, slow and cheap).

CLIMATE (see also pp. 60-63)

India can be conveniently divided into three climatic zones: the north, the south and the hill regions, and into three distinctive seasons: the winter, the summer and monsoon. The best time to plan your trip to India is from mid-September to early April, except for Kashmir, which is best from April to September, or the hill stations, which are good at any time in the summer except during the monsoon.

The monthly average maximum and minimum daytime temperatures* in degrees Fahrenheit are:

		J	F	M	A	M	J	J	A	S	O	N	D
Bombay	max.	83	83	86	89	91	89	85	85	85	89	89	87
	min.	67	67	72	76	80	79	77	76	76	76	73	69
Calcutta	max.	80	84	93	97	96	92	89	89	90	89	84	79
	min.	55	59	69	75	77	79	79	78	78	74	64	55
Delhi	max.	70	75	87	97	105	102	96	93	93	93	84	73
	min.	44	49	58	68	79	83	81	79	75	65	52	46
Madras	max.	85	88	91	95	101	100	96	95	94	90	85	84
	min.	67	68	72	78	82	81	79	78	77	75	72	69

And in degrees Celsius:

		J	F	M	A	M	J	J	A	S	O	N	D
Bombay	max.	28	28	30	32	33	32	29	29	29	32	32	31
	min.	19	19	22	24	27	26	25	24	24	24	23	21
Calcutta	max.	27	29	34	36	36	33	32	32	32	32	29	26
	min.	13	15	21	24	25	26	26	26	26	24	18	13
Delhi	max.	21	24	31	36	41	39	36	34	34	34	29	23
	min.	7	9	14	20	26	28	27	26	24	18	11	8
Madras	max.	29	31	33	35	38	38	36	35	34	32	29	29
	min.	19	20	22	26	28	27	26	26	25	24	22	21

* Minimum temperatures are measured just before sunrise, maximum temperatures in the afternoon.

COMMUNICATIONS (see also Hours)

Telephone and Telegrams. India is in the process of modernizing its telephone system, raising great hopes for the future. In the meantime, however, many city numbers, particularly in Delhi, Bombay and Madras, are being altered to suit new telephone exchanges. Before calling, check whether the exchange code, the first couple of digits in your number, are still correct.

Direct dialling is possible between major cities. Where you make a call through the operator, you'll have to book a few hours in advance. There are three basic types of call: *ordinary, urgent* and *lightning*. A Delhi-Bombay *lightning* call might take an hour to materialize, sometimes more, and will cost more than a call of similar duration from Delhi to New York!

Likewise, the inter-city telegram service is frequently disrupted by line failure. Public telex is often the best way of reaching a contact in another part of the country.

On the international side, extensive satellite links can put you through to almost anywhere in the world with a service that is up to international standards.

You can book both domestic and international telephone calls through the hotel switchboard or at the nearest PTO (Post and Telegraph Office), or use the direct dialling booths. Big cities have a 24-hour telephone and telex service at the central PTO. India also has reverse charges (collect) agreements with most countries.

Postal Service. The postal service within India and abroad is generally very reliable. An airmail letter usually takes up to seven days to Europe or the US. Stamps are sold at post offices and in some large hotel receptions. It is best to watch your letters being franked rather than using public letter boxes. Lower denomination stamps and envelopes tend not to stick very well, hence the pot of glue on all counters. You can send bulkier souvenirs home by surface mail, but you must first have the package cleared by customs.

CRIME AND THEFT

One wouldn't really expect to recover a camera left behind on a park bench anywhere in the world; India is no exception to this rule. However, your valuables are probably less vulnerable in India than in many parts of the West. Common sense precautions go a long way towards guaranteeing a safe journey, but don't leave valuables lying around, avoid being obvious – a few hundred dollars can mean a year's earnings to many people!

Violence against foreigners is virtually unheard of in India, and it is probably safer to walk the streets of Delhi late at night than it is in many places back home.

CUSTOMS, ENTRY AND EXIT REGULATIONS

Visas. All travellers, including citizens from Commonwealth countries, need visas. There are three kinds of visa: *entry, tourist* and *transit*.

Entry visas apply to those frequently travelling to India on business assignments; they can be extended.

Transit visas have a maximum duration of 15 days and are only needed if you are merely making a stop-over and want to leave the airport. They are granted to passengers who have tickets for onward destinations. Two-way transit visas can also be obtained.

Tourist visas are normally valid for three months and can only be extended at the Government's of India's discretion. You must arrive in India within six months of the visa date of issue, or it will automatically become void.

For a tourist visa, you will need three passport-size photos and, unless you hold a passport from a fee-exempt country, you will be expected to pay for it. Tour organizers can arrange for group visas.

Arrival (see also AIRPORTS). Tourists are allowed to bring in all the usual paraphernalia they normally carry with them. Certain high value items, however, will be entered in your passport by the customs officials, but if you are thinking of returning to India on the same passport, insist that the customs officers cancel these entries. Any items which have been written into passport cannot be sold and have to be shown on departure. In case of loss or theft, you will need a police document which proves that you have reported the incident.

Fire-arms and habit-forming drugs are banned and so is the import of gold bullion and electronic items for commercial purposes.

Departure. When leaving India, you are allowed to take with you all kinds of souvenirs, provided they are not recognized antiques (this is defined as any items which are over 99 years old) – it is always best to keep your sales receipt with you to appease any over-zealous customs officers. Please note that you may not export any kind of animal skin other than a small amount of cow leather and a few peacock feathers. You should steer clear of tiger-skin rugs and snake skins.

The following chart shows the allowances made for certain duty-free items that you may take into India and, when returning, into your own country. Check them out before you leave, rather than running into any major problems at than airport.

	Cigarettes	Cigars		Tobacco	Liquor		Wine
India	200	or	50	or 250g.		0.95 l	
Australia	200	or	250g. or	250g.	1 l.	or	1 l.
Canada	200	and	50 and	900g.	1.1 l.	or	1.1 l.
Eire	200	or	50 or	250g.	1 l.	and	2 l.
N. Zealand	200	or	50 or	250g.	1.1 l.	and	4.5 l.
S. Africa	400	and	50 and	250g.	1 l.	and	2 l.
U.K.	200	or	50 or	250g.	1 l.	and	2 l.
U.S.A.	200	and	100 and	*	1 l.	and	1 l.

* A reasonable quantity

Currency restrictions. It is forbidden to take Indian rupees into or out of the country. There is, however no limit set on the total amount of foreign currencies you can bring into India, providing you declare amounts in excess of U.S.$1,000 on arrival. Foreign currencies which total the amount imported and declared may be exported.

E ELECTRIC CURRENT
Electricity supply in all tourist areas and big cities is a standard 220 AC, 50 cycles. Only a few remote parts of northern India are still using DC. During the summer months especially, the voltage can fluctuate wildly, so avoid plugging in delicate systems directly without the use of a voltage stabilizer. Take spare batteries with you, especially the 9V type which can be difficult to obtain.

EMBASSIES, HIGH COMMISSIONS AND CONSULATES
Most countries have diplomatic ties with India with an embassy or high commission in New Delhi and a consulate in Bombay, Calcutta or Madras.

Australia   *High Commission*: 1/50 Shanti Path, Chanakyapuri, New Delhi 110021; tel. 601406, and 601336.
Consulate: Maker Towers, 'E' Block, 16th Floor, Cuffe Parade, Colaba, Bombay 400005; tel. 2181071/72.

Canada   *High Commission:* 7/8 Shanti Path, Chanakyapuri, New Delhi 110021; tel. 6876500.

Consulate: 41-45 Maker Chambers, VI, 4th Floor,
6 Jamna Lal Bajaj Marg, Nariman Point, Bombay
400021; tel. 2876027/29.

New Zealand   50-N Nyaya Marg, Chanakyapuri, New Delhi
110021; tel. 6883170.

UK   *High Commission*: Shanti Path, Chanakyapuri,
New Delhi 110021; tel. 601371.
Consulates: Maker Chambers, IV, 2nd Floor,
222 Jamna Lal Bajaj Marg, Nariman Point,
Bombay 400021; tel. 2830517.
1 Ho Chi Minh Sarani, Calcutta 700071;
tel. 2425171.
24 Anderson Road, Madras 600006; tel. 8273136/37.

USA   *Embassy*: Shanti Path, Chanakyapuri, New Delhi
110021; tel. 600651.
Consulates: Lincoln House, 78 Bhulabhai Desai
Road, Bombay 400026; tel. 3633611.
5/1 Ho Chi Minh Sarani, Calcutta 700071; tel. 223611.
Mount Road, Madras 600006; tel. 473040.

GETTING TO INDIA   G

Due to the complexity and variability of the many fares, you should ask the
advice of an informed travel agent well before your departure.

Scheduled Flights

All major international airlines land at Delhi and Bombay (see under AIR-
PORTS); some also fly to Calcutta and Madras. Approximate flying times:
London–Delhi 11½ hours; New York–Delhi 19 hours.

Charter Flights and Package Tours

From North America: India is extensively featured on a number of tours
from the United States, but it is always combined with another country
such as Nepal, China or Japan. There are no package tours from Canada.

From the United Kingdom: A wide variety of tours is offered, with
air/hotel packages to Bombay, Calcutta, Delhi, Goa, Jaipur, Kovalam,
Madras and Udaipur. There are also tours available which take in two or
more Indian cities, while some combine India with another country such as
Nepal or Sri Lanka.

From Australia and New Zealand: India is sometimes featured on Asian tours, but these are not frequent.

Overland

It is possible to cross into India by land from both Nepal and Bangladesh although the journey can be somewhat strenuous: by bus from Kathmandu to Dehli; or by bus from Dhaka to the Bangladesh border, then by train to Calcutta. Both routes take a minimum of two or three days. Since the recent turmoil in the western state of Punjab, foreigners are not allowed to travel by land from Pakistan.

H HEALTH AND MEDICAL CARE (see also pp. 63-64)

Before travelling to India, you are advised to take out a personal health insurance to cover possible mishaps. Most insurance companies provide this service.

Likewise, consult your family doctor for a routine check-up and ask him to prescribe medication for potential stomach upsets. Anti-malaria tablets must be taken at least two weeks before departure and for six weeks upon returning home. Remember also to pack a small bottle of light wound disinfectant.

Most people during the course of their stay in India will contract some form of stomach trouble. In most cases, it is nothing to worry about, being more of an irritant than anything else. The remedy is simple: avoid rich, spicy food for a while, double-check drinking water (be sure to avoid tap water), peel all the fruit you eat and take medication if required. Bottled mineral water is widely available in the cities, but may be difficult to obtain in the smaller towns. Stock up whenever possible.

Due to the dramatic weather changes between seasons, people can catch heavy colds at any time to the year. Carrying tablets therefore that combat flu symptoms will help. Dust may cause conjunctivitis, so soothing eye drops will come in handy. Sensitive skins also need to be protected against the sun. Bring insect repellent and an anti-irritant for insect bites. High levels of heat can cause outbursts of prickly heat (use talcum powder) and migraines. Take plenty of liquids and mineral salts to combat dehydration.

Although not mandatory, vaccinations against tuberculosis, hepatitis, hepatitis, and tetanus may be worth it. A valid yellow fever certificate is mandatory for those from South America, Africa and other areas where there is yellow fever.

While in India steer completely clear of stray mammals – particularly dogs – because there is a risk of rabies.

Cities like Delhi and Bombay have Western-style clinics, your embassy in New Delhi can recommend one. Government hospitals are cheap, but if you are going to have injections done here, insist that the doctor either uses a disposable needle or that the sterilization process is done in front of you. This is for your own peace of mind.

HOURS

All central government offices, except post offices, railways, etc., follow a five-day week, closing on Saturdays and Sundays.

Most **markets** close one day each week; the day varies from place to place. **Shops** generally open at 10am and close by 8pm; some are shut for lunch.

Administrative **offices** (other than central railway and airline offices) only start becoming active by about 11 am and will be devoid of life by 5.30pm The official lunch-break is from 1.30 to 2pm. Station booking-counters open with the first trains.

Banks dealing with foreign currency open from 10.30am to 2.30pm on weekdays, and from 10.30am to 12.30pm on Saturdays, however, on Saturdays it may be difficult to change your traveller's cheques outside the main cities.

Post offices open at 9.30am, closing at 5.30pm in larger places and 3.30pm elsewhere. Getting there early to avoid the crowds isn't always the best idea – you might have to wait some time for the staff to arrive! In major cities, the main telephone and telex office generally provides a round-the-clock service.

Museums and **parks** close by 5 or 5.30pm, (but you should check which day they close).

Hairdressers in large hotels will take clients in the early evening.

LANGUAGE (see also USEFUL EXPRESSIONS)   **L**

Hindi, based on Sanskrit and which is akin to many European languages, is the official national language of India, but each State also has its own regional language – one of the 15 listed in the Constitution. English is still used alongside Hindi for official purposes.

People in north India generally speak Hindi, while in the south, where the regional languages are Dravidian, you'll find more English spoken.

M MAPS

Good road maps of the Indian subcontinent are published in Europe and the US Indian tourist offices hand out useful maps and brochures.

Street maps are not always available but your best bet will be the local tourist office or your hotel reception desk. Street maps of big cities, like Delhi and Bombay, can be purchased from newspaper stands but can be a little misleading.

The maps in this book were prepared by Falk-Verlag, Hamburg.

MEETING PEOPLE

All transactions and most social encounters in India begin with the well established ritual of exchanging visiting cards.

Like everywhere else, politeness in India is considered to be a virtue. You'll quickly find that most Indians will go out of their way to be friendly and helpful to you.

A traveller will frequently be asked about his nationality, name, marital status and children, though the limited spread of English tends to restrict the scope of most conversations to simple things. It can be a bit tedious to go around like a walking curriculum vitae, but just keep smiling. This quaint curiosity is built on the best of friendly intentions, and it is part of India's charm.

No topics of conversation are taboo, providing you don't take up an intransigent or arrogant stand. On the contrary, Indians are extremely eager to explain their country and their beliefs to foreigners, which could make for interesting conversation.

Indians seldom shake hands when greeting people, other than during the course of official business; instead, you'll soon learn to *namasté* with both hands brought together at face level.

Many Indians are teetotal and/or vegetarian, so that if you are inviting someone out for a meal, it would be a good idea to inquire beforehand about tastes and preferences.

MONEY MATTERS (see also Hours)

Currency. The Indian unit of currency is the *rupee* (abbreviated *Rs*), which is divided into 100 *paise*. There are coins of 5, 10, 20, 25, 50 paise and of 1, 2 and 5 rupees. Banknotes exist in denominations of 1, 2, 5, 10, 20, 50, 100 and 500 rupees.

Indians are rather fussy about the condition of their paper notes. A shopkeeper often turns down a note because it is very slightly torn at the edge while accepting another one with a great big hole in the middle! There is indeed the very much mistaken belief that the Reserve Bank of India has ruled that torn-at-the-edge notes are worthless. All the same, you should still check your change carefully every time you pay for or purchase something, and you should refuse any frayed and dirty notes you may be offered as change. Don't even try to mend notes with transparent sticky tape – they are unacceptable in this form.

There is a chronic shortage of small cash and many shopkeepers give out sweets or stamps by way of change. Taxi and motor-rickshaw drivers are also notoriously without adequate change and you might often find yourself having to pay a little more just to break up a roadside deadlock. When cashing in your foreign exchange in a large bank, it would therefore be a good idea to ask to have part of your Indian money given to you in small notes. Some banks give extremely valuable wads of a hundred notes of Rs1 or 2. Hang on to the bank receipts since these will allow you to cash in your excess rupees on departure.

Please note that it is a criminal offence to change money on the black market, and so this activity is best avoided.

Traveller's cheques can be cashed in at most banks and in many hotels, though in the latter case it may be at a slightly inferior rate. Some shops are also authorized to deal in foreign exchange.

Credit cards and personal cheques. The use and acceptability of credit cards is becoming increasingly widespread in India now. All big hotels and government emporiums recognize them, and so do many shops and restaurants. Personal cheques, however, will find few takers, although some foreign banks will help you out providing you can produce a foreign resident in India who will stand as surety.

NEWSPAPERS AND MAGAZINES

English-language newspapers, both national and regional, are widespread throughout the country. There is a large number of English-language news magazines, some of which are absolute musts for those interested in the intricacies of Indian political and social life.

Most of the major cities now have a weekly *What's On* type of magazine (available from bookstalls), which gives the opening and closing times for museums and information on current cultural events.

P PACKING

While most things are easily available in large Indian towns, there are still certain items you'll be relieved to have with you.

Other than essential medicines (see HEALTH AND MEDICAL CARE), think of packing in your luggage the following items: a drinking-water bottle; a pocket torch (flashlight); a padlock if you are thinking of staying in a few cheaper hotels (digital padlocks spare the worry of losing the key) or if you are going to travel a lot on Indian railways; a penknife (but don't board planes with it in your cabin luggage); water-purifying tablets; a money-belt and half a dozen passport size photos of yourself – which come in useful if you are applying for permits to Darjeeling or Sikkim or for a rail pass. A universal plug for wash basins will come in handy more often than you might imagine! If batteries are found in your cabin luggage on board a plane, they will be confiscated.

Aspirin is readily available, but you might like to have your own favourite brand handy. Also, don't forget to pack some sterile cotton wool and adhesive bandages and last, but not least, toilet paper or paper tissues (found only in large Indian towns).

Sewing kits can be useful, but in every hotel there will be somebody to do the job for you; if not, on every pavement there is at least one tailor or one cobbler capable of performing instant miracles for a few rupees.

Take a washing powder or liquid detergent if you are thinking of doing your own laundry, although there will nearly always be a *dhobi* laundry service available.

Pack a cloth hat to protect you against the sun, as well as sensible light cotton clothes to wear during the hot and monsoon seasons, a swimsuit, and a pullover for cold spells during the winter months or if you are going to the hills (see also CLIMATE).

When travelling long distances by rail, a bed-sheet can make a lot of difference to your comfort and so will a plastic or aluminium mug, which will allow you to drink tea, bought on the platform, when the train moves off. Ear plugs can sometimes be a life-saving device, particularly at night in crowded compartments or in a bus with non-stop Indian film music (often distorted) blaring out of the public address system. A short-wave transistor radio will enable you to keep in touch with world affairs.

Finally, you might also like to bring with you a few small gifts for people who have been particularly helpful and shown you hospitality. Any small item with a foreign trademark on it will be happily accepted; this could be disposable gas lighters, ball point and coloured felt-tip pens, stamps from your own country, cigarettes, picture postcards, perfume samples, etc. In many places you might find yourself surrounded by swarms of children clamouring for 'school pens, stamps and coins'.

PHOTOGRAPHY

Colour print and black-and-white films are readily available in the main cities, but film for slides is not easy to find in India. Some shops in big cities do stock E6 preparations (Agfachrome, Fujichrome, etc.) but retail prices are about three times what they are in Europe. Colour-print film and black-and-white rolls are more common.

Delhi and Bombay and other larger towns have plenty of photo studios which can process black-and-white or colour film. Generally the quality is good, but prints are usually postcard size only. It is perhaps best to take the film back home with you and have it processed there.

Customs impose a limit of five rolls of film per person. Although all metal detector machines are said to be film-safe, you might feel happier, when passing airport security checks, to carry your film in a clear plastic bag you'll hand over to the security staff for inspection.

India is a colourful country and your right hand index finger will be itching on the shutter trigger of your camera from the moment you arrive. There are, however, certain things which can't be photographed: military installations, as well as bridges of all sorts, airports and railway stations, power stations and refineries, dams and telephone exchanges. Likewise, it is always best to get permission to photograph anyone.

PLANNING YOUR TRIP

Most of India is open to foreign travel, with the exception of the territories of Assam, Arunachal Pradesh, Nagaland, Manipur, Mizoram, Tripura and Meghalaya. There is also an 'inner-line' exclusion zone running along the frontier between India and China. People wishing to trek in Kashmir and Ladakh, as well as parts of Darjeeling and Sikkim, should inquire at the local tourist office before setting off: some hill areas may be completely open, others may need special access permits (see p.155), and others still will be entirely out of bounds.

The FRRO's (Foreigners Regional Registration Office) which can be found in Delhi, Bombay, Calcutta, Madras and other state capitals, come under the umbrella responsibility of the Under Secretary, Home Affairs Ministry, Foreigners Division, Lok Nayak Bhavan, Khan Market, New Delhi 110003. They will be in charge of all visa and permit problems.

POLICE

Traffic police do not carry guns. However, uniforms (on the colourful side) generally vary from state to state. Police forces responsible for law and order are armed, the officers with revolvers and the men with Enfield rifles.

Banks are guarded by armed, retired servicemen. Each locality has one or more police stations or police booths where foreigners can register any complaints they may have.

PRICES

The following are some prices in Indian rupees and US dollars. However, they must be regarded as approximate as inflation is ever present.

Airport departure tax. Rs300 (Rs150 to neighbouring countries).

Car hire. Charged per kilometre from Rs5 for a non-air-conditioned car; from Rs6 upwards for an air-conditioned (AC) Indian car; more will be charged for a luxury imported vehicle; Rs24 upwards per hour waiting charges. Overnight charges for the driver start from Rs125 per night. Remember that all rented cars are chauffeur-driven. In the cities as car may be rented on a flat rate basis, i.e. 4 hours, 40 km Rs200 non-AC Rs300 AC.

Cigarettes. Rs25 for a packet of 20.

Discover India Pass. 21 days U.S.$375.

Hairdresser. From Rs70 for a man's haircut in a luxury hotel; from Rs175 for a woman's shampoo and cut.

Hotels. Double room in a luxury establishment approximately 2,600 per night. Middle of the range hotels from Rs1,000 to Rs1,700 per night for a double, depending on whether it is air-conditioned or not. Local and luxury taxes are a few percent, approximately 5–20% extra, although it is worth knowing that this can depend on the State in which you are travelling.

Indian Airline Discount fares. The Discover India Pass is valid for 21 days and costs US $ 400.

India Wonder Fare. 7 days US$200 (see p.239). Youth fares have a 25% discount for the under 30's.

Indrail Pass. Fares vary from US$70 to US$960 according to the class of accommodation and period of validity.

Meals. A snack meal : Rs30 upwards in a middle-range restaurant; from Rs100 in a luxury hotel. Full meal (Indian style): from Rs150.

Taxis Fares to and from airports are supposed to operate at a fixed rate. Motor-rickshaws start from Rs2.20 per kilometre, double for taxis.

Trains. Delhi to Bombay (approximately 1,400 km; 1000 miles) AC first class Rs2,030, non-AC first class Rs704, AC second class Rs1,170, non-AC second class Rs210, AC chair car Rs580.

PUBLIC HOLIDAYS

Due to the multiplicity of religions in India, public holidays are plentiful and confusing.

Fixed national holidays are set on the following dates: January 26, Republic Day; May 1, Labour Day; August 15, Independence Day; and October 2, Mahatma Gandhi's Birthday. Banks are closed on September 30 and March 31. Other holidays vary according to region. A list of official holidays can be obtained from tourist offices.

RADIO AND TV

All India Radio (AIR) broadcasts on medium wave, with news either in English, Hindi or a regional language.

Indian television provides news in Hindi and English, as well as an array of indigenous films, song and dance programmes, farming, science and sport. Imported films, documentaries, serials and sports programmes are also broadcast. Television (Hong Kong) is also available.

Luxury hotels generally provide a TV set in each room.

RELIGIOUS SERVICES

No other country in the world has such a wealth of faiths as India, reflected in the beautiful architecture of its churches, mosques and shrines.

Access to places of worship is generally open, except for some Hindu temples and all Parsi fire-temples. Mosques are closed to non-Muslims at certain times of day. In most places of worship you'll be asked to take off your shoes and/or cover your head so it might be a good idea to take along some form of head covering to use. You'll find Sikh *gurdwaras* ban the entry of tobacco, while Jain temples forbid anyone entering the premises to bring in any form of leather (including wallets). Therefore, if you wish to take advantage of all the oppportunities for sightseeing, you should consider packing a hip bag or money belt made from canvas or another fabric that would be acceptable.

Synagogues can be found in big cities such as Bombay and Delhi, Christian churches of all kinds exist in practically every town.

RESTAURANTS (see also p.209)

First-class hotels naturally offer sophisticated surroundings and a touch of luxury for the traveller. You will nearly always encounter middle-range restaurants (for both Indian and Chinese food) where the quality of the food and service will vary between good and mediocre; there is no fool-proof way of sorting out the better restaurants before actually sampling the food. Trial is still the best method for judging standards.

Many of the small roadside establishments, unenticing by all Western standards of conviviality, sometimes serve excellent fare for next to nothing, but these are not recommended for the short-stay traveller.

On the Menu

aloo	potato
barfi	sugar and milk sweets
biriani	north Indian rice and meat dish
chai	tea
chapati	unleavened bread, cooked on an open pan or griddle
chawal	rice
dal	lentils or kidney beans
faluda	sweet noodles with milk and ice cream
gosht	meat, generally mutton
halwa	carrot-based or semolina dessert
idli	little dumpling of steamed rice flour, eaten at breakfast with chutney and curry
kebab	barbecued meat
keema	minced meat, generally mutton
kirra	cucumber
kofta	spicy minced-meat balls
korma	a curd-based curry sauce
kulfi	Indian ice-cream
lassi	curd-based milk-shake, sweet or salty
masala	mixed spices
masala dosa	pancake of rice flour and ground lentils with spicy potato filling
mutter	peas
nan	leavened bread
nimbu pani or *nimbu soda*	or fresh lime with water or preferably soda
pakora	deep-fried savoury fritter with onion or potato
paneer	Indian cottage cheese

papad/papadum	crispy spicy wafers
paratha	flaky *chapati*, generally fried in butter and often stuffed
pomfret	type of very fleshy fish
pulao	north Indian rice and meat dish
puri	deep-fried 'bubble' *chapati*
raita	curd (*dahi*) mixed with either tomatoes, green peppers or cucumber
roomali roti	paper-thin *chapati* ('roomal' means handkerchief)
roti	generic name for oven- or pan-cooked bread
sabzi	vegetables
sag	a type of spinach
samosa	deep-fried, stuffed pasties
seer	type of very fleshy fish
tandoori	meat (generally chicken) marinated in spice and curd, cooked in a traditional oven
tikka	pieces of diced meat/fish, marinated and grilled on an open fire

TIME DIFFERENCES

T

Indian Standard Time (IST) is GMT plus 5½ hours, winter and summer alike. The most bizarre time difference in the world exists between India and Nepal: 10 minutes!

	New York	London	**Delhi**	Sydney
January	1.30a.m.	6.30a.m.	**noon**	5.30p.m.
July	2.30a.m.	7.30a.m.	**noon**	4.30p.m.

TIPPING

It is customary to leave a tip of about 10% of the total bill in restaurants. Elsewhere, however, tipping is entirely discouraged by the Government of India. Do not try to tip government employees, although museum guides will invariably give hints at the end of a conducted tour so it will be up to you to decide whether his stories and information are worthy of a tip! In temples, however, it is a different story : the *baksheesh* is more or less mandatory; you should also give a rupee to the person who looked after your shoes while you were visiting.

TOILETS

The toilets in India are generally very, very basic, but all the same, don't shun the 'eastern' (seatless) version, because they are often much more hygienic than the European style. The water tap (faucet) nearby is to wash afterwards.

Tourists will often bless their stock of paper tissues.

TOURIST INFORMATION OFFICES

Indian Tourist Offices at the following addresses will help prepare your trip:

Australia: Level One, 17 Castlereagh Street, Sydney, NSW 2000; tel. (02) 232-1600 and (02) 232-1796.

Canada: 60 Bloor Street, West Suite No 1003, Toronto, Ontario M4W 3B8; tel. 416-962 3787/88.

Japan: Pearl Building, No.9-18 Ginza, 7 Chome, Chuo Ku, Tokyo 104; tel. (03) 571-5062/63.

UK: 7 Cork Street, London, W1X 2AB; tel. 071-437 3677/78.

USA: 30 Rockefeller Plaza, Room 15, North Mezzanine, New York, NY 10112; tel. (212) 586-4901/02/03/04. 3550 Wilshire Boulevard, Suite 204, Los Angeles, CA 90010; tel. (213) 380-8855.

In India the major tourist offices are:

Bombay: 123 M Karve Road, opposite Church Gate; tel. 293144.

Santa Cruz Airport; tel. 6325331.

Calcutta: 'Embassy', 4 Shakespeare Sarani; tel. 221402.

Dum Dum Airport; tel. 572611.

Madras: 154 Anna Salai; tel. 869685 and 869695.

Meenambakam Airport; tel 431686.

New Delhi: 88 Janpath, New Delhi 110001; tel. 3320005. Indira Gandhi International Airport; tel. 391171. Domestic Airport; tel. 3295296.

Generally, airport tourist offices are open 24 hours, and others from 9am to 6pm only.

TRAVELLING AROUND INDIA (see also p. 64)

Air (see also AIRPORTS). India has an extensive airline network, although flights can sometimes be unreliable. The main problem is booking; many of the more popular routes, such as Delhi-Srinagar, are full-up months in advance. So don't waste time on arrival: as soon as you know where you are going and how you want to get there, book. There are two types of ticket: *confirmed* which are (mostly) trouble-free, and *requested* which frequently only offer a slim chance of travel.

Indian Airlines (IA), the state-owned domestic carrier, offers tourists two discount schemes: a 7-day *India Wonder Fare* (one region only) or a 21-day *Discover India* fare, with unlimited travel, but only one stop in each town. The *Discover India* tickets must be purchased abroad either at Air India offices or at an agreed travel agent. The *India Wonder Fare* can by obtained in India, but must be paid for in foreign currency. Tourists are expected to pay for their tickets in foreign exchange.

In Delhi, the IA office is at Kanchenjunga House, Barakhamba Road, New Delhi 110001; tel. 331-3732 and 331-0517. In Bombay: Air India Building, Nariman Point, Bombay 400 021; tel. 2048585.

There are a number of private airlines operating throughout India, which offer a good standard of service and are well worth considering.

India also has a small feeder-service called *Vayudoot* which links up smaller towns, particularly useful if you are thinking of going to some of the more remote hill stations.

Vayudoot head office is at: Malhotra Building, Connaught Place, New Delhi 110001; tel. 3312779.

Rail. Indian Railways (administratively divided into: Northern, Western, Eastern, Central and Southern railways) have five basic classes of travel: First Class Air Conditioned (AC), Second Class AC, AC Chair, First Class non-AC and Second Class non-AC. During the summer months an AC compartment is best, especially if travelling through the Indian plains.

Other than a few super-de-luxe fast trains, there are three types of train: *Express*, *Mail* and *Passenger*. You should certainly avoid *Passenger* trains which stop at every station no matter how long the journey.

Tourists will find the *Indrail Pass* the best buy if they intend to use the train a lot. These are valid for unlimited travel for 7–90 days. Pass holders have a priority booking allowance at most stations. *Indrail Passes* can be purchased abroad through approved travel agents. You can buy them in India from approved travel agents and at special railway-station booking counters for tourists in Delhi, Bombay, Calcutta, Madras, Goa, Bangalore,

Varanasi, Agra, Ahmadabad, Aurangabed, Chandigar, Gorakhpur, Jaipur and Hyderbad, Jaipur, Trivandram, Amritsar, Rameswaran and Vadodara.

All long-distance trains have sleepers. Second Class non-AC berths are wooden planks; First Class and AC berths are cushioned. Second Class berths, whether AC or not, give straight onto the main corridor, but First Class berths are separate compartments with slide-doors and catch-locks.

In First Class and AC, you can hire sheets and blankets (nights can be chilly in AC even in the summer).

Bring plenty of books, fruit and drinking water. You will marvel at the ability of Indian travellers to emerge from a 48-hour journey as fresh as when they started, while you will be in dire need of soap and water.

Food is served on Indian trains. Apart from one or two luxury trains, there won't be much of a choice (generally it will simply be a question of vegetarian or non-vegetarian) and will consist of a *thali* or a cardboard box filled with plastic bags of curry and rice.

For booking tickets, foreigners need their passports.

Road. Where there's no railway (e.g. parts of Rajasthan), there'll be a road and dozens of inter-city buses. The fares are low and so is the comfort! Buses on routes, like Agra and Srinagar are plush and classy.

Discovering India by car is best, and cars are hired chauffeur-driven.

U USEFUL EXPRESSIONS

Hindi is spoken mainly in the north of the country. Here are some useful words and expressions to listen out for and use. Verbs ending with a '-yé' sound are polite imperatives, but those ending with a '-o' are familiar forms of address. The '-ji' suffix is a polite honorific. A wavy line over a vowel indicates a nasal sound.

Yes	ji hā
No	nah
Please	meher bāni
Thank you	dhanyavād (sometimes 'shukriyā' in northern India)
Beg your pardon/sorry	māf (or shama) kijiyé
Hello/welcome/goodbye	namasté
How are you?	kyā hāl hai/āp kaisé haı
I'm fine.	thik hai
I don't understand.	samjhā nahı
Tomorrow/yesterday	kal (confusion is possible)

Today	āj
Tonight	āj rāt ko
This morning	āj subhā
This evening	āj shām ko
Good	achchā
Excellent/well done	shābāsh
Fast/early	jaldi
Slow/late	dhiré
Money	pāisā
How much is it?	kyā dām hai
It is very expensive.	yé bahut mahinga hai
Are you free? (taxi, rickshaw)	kyā āp khāli haı
How far is it?	kitni dūr hai
Where is it?	kahā hai
On your right	dãy
On your left	bãy
Straight ahead	sidha
Please stop here.	yahā rokiyé
Please go faster.	jaldi chaliyé
Please go slowly.	dhiré chaliyé
Please go away.	jāiyé
Go away!	jāo
Let's go!	chalo (polite form chaliyé)
Please bring	lāiyé
Please give	dijiyé
I'm not feeling well.	maı kuchch bimār hū
I need a doctor.	mujko doctor chaiyé
This is not good.	yé achchā nahıhai
It is very good.	bahut achchā hai
It is very hot.	bahut garam hai
It is very cold.	bahut thandā hai
It is very beautiful.	yé bahut sunder hai
Please give me some water.	mujko pani dijiyé
This is not clean.	yé saf nahı hai

NUMBERS

1	ek	12	barah
2	do	20	bis
3	tin	30	tis
4	char	40	chalis
5	panch	50	pachās
6	chhé	60	sāth
7	sat	70	sattar
8	ath	80	assi
9	nau	90	nabbé
10	dass	100	sau
11	gyarah	1,000	hazār

The following two are fairly important since they are not only typically Indian but also occur frequently in the press, and on official documents etc.

100,000	lakh (written: 1,00,000)
10,000,000	crore (1,00,00,000)

W WEIGHTS AND MEASURES

India uses the metric system everywhere.

Temperature

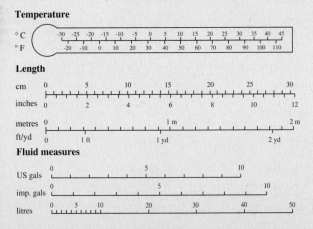

Length

Fluid measures

242

Weight

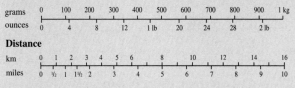

grams	0	100	200	300	400	500	600	700	800	900	1 kg
ounces	0		4		8		12		1 lb		20		24		28		2 lb

Distance

km	0	1	2	3	4	5	6	8	10	12	14	16
miles	0	½	1	1½	2	3	4	5	6	7	8	9	10

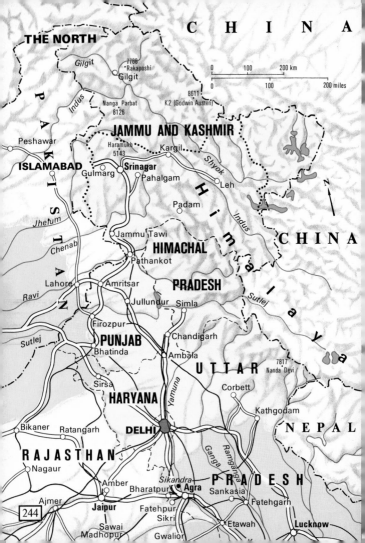

CHINA

THE NORTH

Gilgit

7788
•Rakaposhi
○Gilgit

| 0 | 100 | 200 km |
| 0 | 100 | 200 miles |

8611
K2 (Godwin Austen)

Nanga Parbat
8126

Indus

JAMMU AND KASHMIR

Haramukh
5143 •••••••• Kargil

○Peshawar

Shyok

ISLAMABAD

Gulmarg ○ **Srinagar**
Pahalgam ○Leh

P A K I S T A N

Jhelum

Padam

Indus

CHINA

N

Chenab

○Jammu Tawi

HIMACHAL

Pathankot○

Ravi

Lahore○ ○Amritsar

PRADESH

○Jullundur Simla○

Sutlej

○Firozpur

H i m a l a y a

PUNJAB Chandigarh○

Bhatinda○ ○Ambala

U T T A R

Sutlej

7817
Nanda Devi

○Sirsa

HARYANA

Yamuna

Corbett○

○Kathgodam

○Bikaner ○Ratangarh

●**DELHI**

N E P A L

R A J A S T H A N

Ganga

Ramganga

○Nagaur

P R A D E S H

Amber○ *Sikandra*
Bharatpur○ ●**Agra**

Sankasia○

244

○Ajmer

○**Jaipur** Fatehpur
Sikri○

○Fatehgarh

Sawai
Madhopur ○Etawah **Lucknow**●

Gwalior○

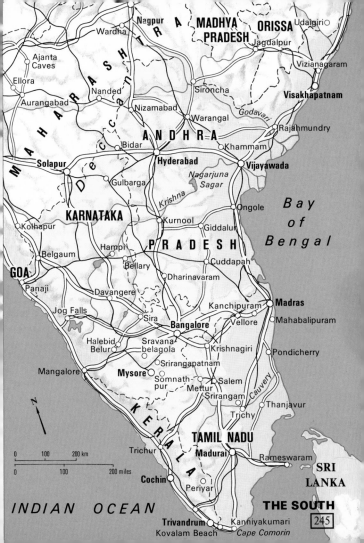

THE EAST

N

| 0 | 100 | 200 km |
| 0 | 100 | 200 miles |

C H I N A

BURMA

Himalaya

ARUNACHAL PRADESH
Kundil
Bazar ○Brahma
Kund
North Lakhimpur
Namdapha

Itanagar

NAGALAND
Kohima

A S S A M
Dispur

MANIPUR
Imphal

MIZORAM
Aizawl
Demagir

MEGHALAYA
Shillong

TRIPURA
Agartala

Brahmaputra

Dhaka

Padma

Mouths of the Ganga

SIKKIM
Gangtok
Timphu

NEPAL

Darjeeling

Katmandu

Motihari

WEST BENGAL
Calcutta
Haldia

Gorakhpur

Ganga

Patna
Nalanda ○Mokameh
Rajgir
Sarnath

BIHAR

Jamshedpur
Ranchi
Keonjhargarh

Paradwip

Lucknow

Sasaram
Bodh Gaya
Gumla
Rourkela

Konorak
Puri

U T T A R   P R A D E S H

Varanasi

Allahabad

Sambalpur
Bhubaneshwar

ORISSA

Fatehgarh
Kanpur

Khajuraho
Rewa

Amarkantak

Saraipali

Udaigiri

M A D H Y A   P R A D E S H

Jabalpur

Mahanadi

Jagdalpur
Vizianagaram

Katni

Raipur

Visakhapatnam

Kanha

247

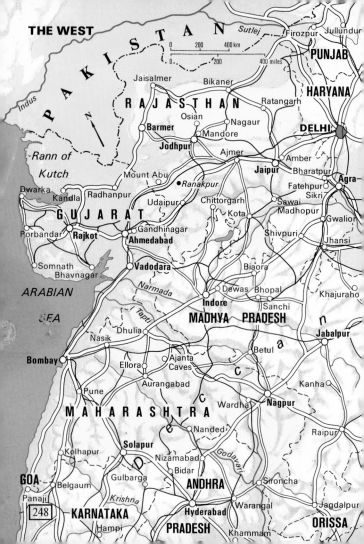

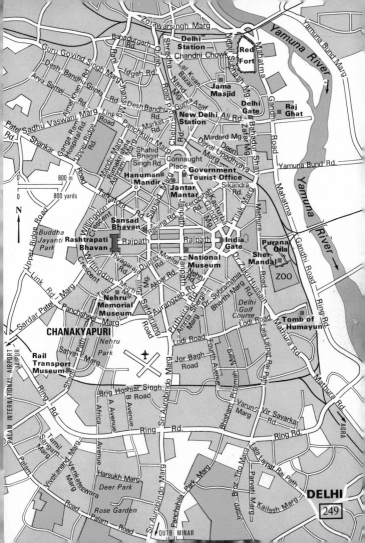

DELHI

249

NASIK, INDORE,
WORLI BUDDHIST
TEMPLE

AIRPORT,
SANTA
CRUZ

POONA

Haines Rd.

Bellasis Rd

Hornby Vellard

Dhobi
Ghat

Clerk
Road

Haines

Victoria and Albert Museum

Victoria
Garden

Zoo

Victoria Rd.

Mahim Bay
Haji Ali's Tomb

BYCULLA

Race Course

Clerk

Arthur Road

Ambedkar Road

Mount Rd.

Love Lane

Reay Rd.

Bombay

Nesbit Road

MAZAGAON

Mahalaxmi
Temple

Central
Station

Dr. Anandrao
Nair Rd.

Victoria Garden Road

Wadi Bunder
Rd.

Bhulabhai Desai (Warden) Rd.

Tardeo Rd.

Bellasis
Road

Duncan
Road

Babula
Tank Rd.

D'Mello
Road

Bombay Docks

TARDEO

Falkland
Road

Grant Road

Rehman Road

Sardar Patel Road

Argyle
Road

Cambala
Road

Peddar
Road

Foras
Road

Masjid Bunder
Rd.

Gowalia
Tank Rd.

Sardar Patel Road

Vithalbhai
Rd.

GIRGAUM

Mumbadevi Temple

Carnac Rd.

D'Mello Road

Harvey Rd.

Hughes
Rd.

Girgaum
Rd.

Hardware Road

Cotton Exchange

Cross
Island

Towers
of Silence

Gibbs Road

Devi
Street

Kalba

Dadabhai Naoroji Road

Elephanta
Caves

Hanging
Gardens

Statue
of Tilak

Netaji Subhash Road

Aquarium

Carnac Rd.

Crawford Market

Kamala
Nehru Park

Queen's
Road

Cruickshank
Rd.

Victoria
Terminus Station

Nepean Sea Road

Ridge Road

Walkeshwar Road

Marine Drive

New Marine Rd.

Gandhi Rd.

Mangalore Rd.

General
Post Office

Jain Temple

Handloom
House

Mole Station

Ballard Rd.

FORT

Back Bay

Government of India
Tourist Office

St. Thomas
Cathedral

Mint

Town Hall,
Central Library

Walkeshwar
Temple

Churchgate Station

Flora Fountain

Rajabai Tower

Raj Bhavan,
Government House

D'Watcha
Rd.

Queen's Road

Jehangir Art Gallery

Prince of Wales
Museum

Sachivalaya

Mayo
Road

Madame Cama Road

Statue of Sivaji

Malabar Point

Gateway
of India

N

0   400   800 m

0   400   800 yards

COLABA

Coffee Parade Rd.

Colaba Rd.

Colaba

ST. JOHN'S CHURCH

BOMBAY

250

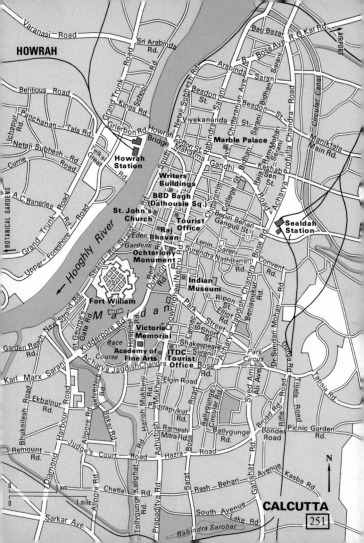

HOWRAH

Varanasi - Road

Sri Arabinda Rd.

Belilious Road

Panchanan Tala Rd.

Ichapur Rd.

Netaji Subhash Rd.

Currie Rd.

A.C. Banerjee Rd.

Grand Trunk Road

Kings Rd.

School Rd.

Grierbon Rd.

Telkal Ghat

Grand Trunk Road

Upper - Foreshore Rd.

Garden Reach Rd.

Karl Marx Saran

Ekbalpur Rd.

Bhukailash Rd.

Harbour Rd.

Remount Rd.

Diamond Rd.

Judge's Court Road

Sarkar Ave.

BOTANICAL GARDENS

Hooghly River

Howrah Station

Howrah Bridge

Howrah Cotton St.

South Mahatma

Strand Rd.

Writers Buildings

BBD Bagh (Dalhousie Sq.)

St. John's Church

Raj Bhavan

Tourist Office

Eden Gardens

Ochterlony Monument

Red Rd.

Dufferin Rd.

Fort William

M a i d a n

Kidderpore Rd.

St. George's Gate Rd.

Belvedere Rd.

Baker Rd.

Alipore Rd.

Chetla Rd.

Tollygunge Kalighat Rd.

Prapadiya Rd.

Bag Bazar

R G Kar Rd.

AIRPORT

Bose Ave.

Sarani

Arabinda Saran

Beadon St.

Rabindra Chandra Road

Circular Canal

Maniktala Main Rd.

Netaji Subhash

Vivekananda Rd.

Beadon Sarani

Bidhan Sarani

Chittaranjan Ave.

Ram Mohan Sarani

Marble Palace

Mahatma Gandhi

Rabindra Sarani

College St.

Bepin Behari Ganguli St.

Keshab Sen St.

Raja Ben St.

Bose Road

Acharya Profulla Chandra Road

Sealdah Station

Lenin Sarani

Surendra Nath Banerji

Chowringhee Nehru Rd.

Indian Museum

Ripon St.

Elliot Rd.

Convent Rd.

Chandra Rd.

Beniapukur Rd.

Victoria Memorial

Academy of Fine Arts

Race Course

Hospital Rd.

Park Street

Carnac St.

Short St.

Shakespeare Sarani

ITDC Tourist Office

Acharya Jagdish Chandra Bose Rd.

Elgin Road

Harish Mukherji Rd.

Paddapukur Rd.

Ramesh Mitra Rd.

Ashutosh Mukherji Rd.

Hazra Road

Sarat Rd.

Rash - Behari Avenue

Lake Rd.

South Avenue

Rabindra Sarobar

Ballygunge Circular Rd.

Ballygunge Rd.

Syed Amir Ali Ave.

Broad St.

Rifle Rd.

Bondel Road

Park Circus

Dr. Sundari Mohan Rd.

Durga Rd.

TilJala Road

Tansia Rd.

Picnic Garden Rd.

Gariahat Rd.

Kasba Rd.

N

0 1 km
1 mile

CALCUTTA

251

NELLORE

GEORGE TOWN

Railway
Station

Railway
Station

Wall Tax

Tirupalli
Str.

PURASAWALKAM

Zoo

People's
Park

Pothan's Broadway

Armenian Street

Thumbu Chetti Street

Narayana Mudali Street

Govind Appa Naicken Street

Angappa Naicken Str.

North Beach Road

Harbour

Railway
Station

General Post Office

Stadium

Broadway
Bus Terminus

Chander Bose Rd.

High Court and
Lighthouse

Town Hall

VEPERY

Central
Railway
Station

S. H. South

Radio Rd.

Railway Station

Fort St. George
Museum

St. Mary's Church

General Road

Hospital Road

Poonamallee High Rd.

Railway
Station

Napier
Park

Government
Museum

CHET PUT.

Connemara
Museum

National Art Gallery

Cooum River

Rajaji Hall

Madras University

Senate House

Chepauk Palace

Air India

Government of India
Tourist Office

Marina
Swimming Pool
Aquarium

Whites Road

TRIPLICANE

South Beach Road

Parthasarathi
Temple

Peters Road

Dr. Besant Rd.

Lloyds Road

Lloyds Road

Music Academy

Edward Elliots Road

Canal

Luz Church

Nageswara
Rao Park

252 **MYLAPORE**

Kapaleeswarar Temple

San Thomé Cathedral

MAHABALIPURAM

MADRAS

B
a
y

o
f

B
e
n
g
a
l

N

0   500 m

0   500 yards

INDEX

An asterisk (*) next to a page number indicates a map reference. Where there is more than one set of page references, the one in bold type refers to the main entry. States listed are in italics. For index to Practical Information, see also pp. 218-219.